# INSIGHTS FOR TODAY

# INSIGHTS FOR TODAY

## A High-Beginning Reading Skills Text

Lorraine C. Smith and Nancy Nici Mare

English Language Institute, Queens College,
The City University of New York

Illustrations by Joseph Tenga

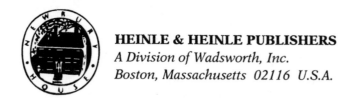

**HEINLE & HEINLE PUBLISHERS**
*A Division of Wadsworth, Inc.*
*Boston, Massachusetts 02116 U.S.A.*

Publisher: Stanley J. Galek
Editor: Erik Gundersen
Associate Editor: Lynne Telson Barsky
Editorial Production Manager: Elizabeth Holthaus
Production Editor: Kristin M. Thalheimer
Photo Coordinator: Martha Leibs-Heckly
Manufacturing Coordinator: Jerry Christopher
Production Coordination and Composition: Caliber/Phoenix Color Corp.
Photographer: Joseph Tenga
Interior Design: Caliber/Phoenix Color Corp.
Cover Design: Christi Rosso

Manufactured in the United States of America

Heinle & Heinle Publishers is a division of Wadsworth, Inc.

## Library of Congress Cataloging-in-Publication Data

Smith, Lorraine C.
    Insights for today : a high-beginning reading skills text / Lorraine C. Smith and Nancy Nici Mare ; illustrations by Joseph Tenga.
        p.    cm.
    Includes index.
    ISBN 0-8384-3978-0
    1. English language--Textbooks for foreign speakers.
    2. Readers--1950-    I. Mare, Nancy Nici, 1957-    . II. Title.
    PE1128.S583   1993
    428.6'4--dc20                                                    92-31760
                                                                          CIP

10  9  8  7  6  5

To Steven

# Contents

# Preface

*Insights for Today* is a reading skills text intended for high-beginning, college-bound students of English as a second or foreign language. The topics in this text are fresh, timely, and multicultural in nature. The readings and activities in this text are designed to take students from a general topic to their own customs, culture, and history.

*Insights for Today* is one in a series of reading skills tests. The complete series has been designed to meet the needs of students from the high-beginning to the advanced levels and includes the following:

- *Insights for Today* . . . High-beginning
- *Issues for Today* . . . Intermediate
- *Concepts for Today* . . . High-intermediate
- *Topics for Today* . . . Advanced

*Insights for Today* provides students with essential practice in the type of reading skills they will need in an academic environment. The book requires students not only to read text, but also to extract basic information from charts, graphs, illustrations, and photographs. Beginning-level students are rarely exposed to this type of reading material.

This thematically-organized text consists of six units, each one containing two chapters that deal with a related subject. This organization gives the instructor the option of either completing entire units or choosing individual chapters as a focus in class. If the teacher chooses to do both chapters, there is a discussion question at the end of each unit that synthesizes aspects of the two related topics.

The illustrations and initial exercise preceding each reading encourage learners to think about the ideas, facts, and vocabulary that will be presented in the reading passage. In fact, discussing the illustrations in class helps lower-level students visualize what they are going to read about and gives them cues for the new vocabulary they will encounter. The exercises that follow the reading passage are intended to develop and improve reading proficiency, including the ability to learn new vocabulary from context, and comprehend English sentence structure.

Beginning-level language students need considerable visual reinforcement of ideas and vocabulary. This is why *Insights for Today* contains so many illustrations. This is also why so many of the follow-up activities are of the type that enable the students to manipulate the information in the text as well as the supplemental information. In fact, the teacher may want the students to work at the blackboard on the charts and lists in the activities at the end of the chapters.

Much of the vocabulary is recycled throughout the exercises and activities in any given chapter. Repetition of vocabulary in varied contexts helps the students not only to understand the new vocabulary better, but also to remember it.

As the students work through the text, they will learn and improve reading skills, and develop confidence in their growing English proficiency skills. At the same time, the teacher will be able to observe their steady progress toward skillful, independent reading.

## Acknowledgments

We want to express our appreciation to the students, faculty, staff, and administration of the English Language Institute at Queens College for their help and support. We would also like to thank our new editor at Heinle & Heinle, Erik Gundersen, for smoothing the transition to our new publishing house. Once again, we thank our families and friends for their ongoing faith in us.

# Introduction

## How to Use This Book

Every chapter in this book consists of the following:

- Prereading Preparation
- Reading Passage
- Fact-Finding Exercise
- Information Recall
- Reading Analysis
- Word Forms
- Vocabulary in Context
- Follow-up Activities
- Topics for Discussion and Writing
- Crossword Puzzle
- CLOZE Quiz

There is also a discussion section at the end of each unit that synthesizes the related topics in the two chapters for that unit. An Index of Key Words and Phrases and an Answer Key appear at the end of the book.

The format of each chapter in the book is consistent. Although each chapter can be done entirely in class, some exercises may be assigned for homework. This, of course, depends on the individual teacher's preference as well as on the availability of class time.

## Prereading Preparation

This prereading activity is designed to stimulate student interest, activate background knowledge, and provide preliminary vocabulary for the reading passage itself. The importance of prereading preparation should not be underestimated. Studies have shown the positive effect of prereading preparation in motivating student interest and in enhancing reading comprehension. In fact, prereading discussion has been shown to be more effective in improving reading comprehension than prevocabulary exercises per se. Time should be spent describing and discussing the illustrations as well as discussing the prereading questions. Furthermore, the students should try to relate the topic to their own experience and to predict what they are going to read about.

## The Reading Passage

As the students read the passage for the first time, they should be encouraged to read *ideas*. In English, ideas are formulated and described in groups of words, in sentences, and in paragraphs, not in individual words. After the students read the passage to themselves, the teacher may want to read the passage aloud to the students. At the beginning level, students are very keen on pronunciation and feel that this practice is helpful to them. Moreover, such practice provides the students with an appropriate model for pronunciation and intonation.

## Fact-Finding Exercise

After the first reading, the students will read and respond to the true/false statements. If a statement is false, the students will go back to the passage and find the lines that contain the correct answer. They will then rewrite the statement so that it becomes true. This activity can be done individually or in groups.

## Information Recall

Students should be instructed to read each passage carefully a second time to pay attention to details. After the second reading, they will answer the questions on specific information in the passage, and compare their answers with a classmate's. The pairs of students can then refer back to the passage and check their answers.

## Reading Analysis

The students will read each question and answer it. The first question in this section always refers to the main idea. There are three possible answers. Two are incorrect because they are too general or too narrow. When going over the exercise, the teacher should discuss with the students why the other two answers are incorrect. The rest of this exercise requires the students to think about the meanings of words and phrases, the structure of sentences and paragraphs, and the relationships among ideas. This exercise is very effective when done in groups. It may also be done individually, but group work gives the students an excellent opportunity to discuss possible answers.

## Word Forms

As an introduction to the word form exercises in this book, it is recommended that the teacher first review parts of speech, especially verbs, nouns, adjectives, and adverbs. Teachers should point out each word form's position in a sentence. Students will develop a sense for which part of speech is missing in a given sentence. Teachers should also point out clues to tense and number, and whether an idea is affirmative or negative. The teacher can do the example with the students before the exercise or as an assignment after the exercise is completed. Each section has its own instructions, depending on the particular pattern which is being introduced. For example, in the section containing words which take *-tion* in the noun form, the teacher can explain that in this exercise the students will look at the verb and noun forms of two types of words that use the suffix *-tion* in their noun form. (1) Some words simply add *-tion* to the verb: *suggest, suggestion*; if the word ends in *-e*, the *-e* is dropped first: *produce, production*. (2) Other words drop the final *-e* and add *-ation*: *examine, examination*. This exercise is very effective when done in pairs. After students have a working knowledge of this type of exercise, it can be assigned for homework.

## Vocabulary in Context

This is a fill-in exercise designed to review items from the previous exercises. The vocabulary has been covered either in the questions or in the Reading Analysis section. This exercise can be done for homework as a review or in class as group work.

## Follow-up Activities

This section contains various activities appropriate to the information in the passages. Some activities are designed for pair and small-group work. Students are encouraged to use the information and vocabulary from the passages both orally and in writing. The teacher may also use these questions and activities as home or in-class assignments. The follow-up activities help the students interact with the real world because they require the students to go outside the classroom to interview people or to get specific information. They are not limited to speaking, reading, or learning in the classroom.

## Topics for Discussion and Writing

This section provides ideas or questions for the students to discuss or to work on alone, in pairs, or in small groups. It provides the students with the opportunity to write.

## Crossword Puzzle

Each chapter contains a crossword puzzle, which contains much of the vocabulary used in that chapter. Students can go over the puzzle orally if pronunciation practice with letters is needed. The teacher can have the students spell out their answers in addition to pronouncing the word itself. Students invariably enjoy doing crossword puzzles. They are an enjoyable way to reinforce the vocabulary presented in the various exercises in each chapter, and they require the students to pay attention to correct spelling.

## CLOZE Quiz

The CLOZE exercises are guided and vary throughout the text. In each CLOZE, certain *types* of words are missing. These words may be articles, prepositions, verbs, pronouns, or quantifiers.

## Index of Key Words and Phrases

This section contains words and phrases from all the chapters for easy reference.

## Answer Key

The Answer Key provides the answers for the exercises.

Credits

Special thanks to:

Jackson Hole Wyoming Airline Diner, Jackson Heights, New York

United States Committee for UNICEF (United Nations Children's Fund): Nobel Peace Prize

National Aeronautics and Space Administration

# UNIT I

## Animals —
## Then and Now

# CHAPTER 1

# Elephants: Gentle Giants of the Earth

---

## Prereading Preparation

1. Look at the photograph on the left. Where do these elephants live?
2. Discuss what you know about elephants. For example, what do they eat? How many babies do they have? How long do they live?
3. What do they use their trunks for?
4. What do they use their tusks for?
5. Some people kill them. Do you know why?
6. Read the title of this chapter. What do you think it means?

1    They live with their mothers, sisters, aunts, nieces and
2 nephews, and an old grandmother, who is the head of the fam-
3 ily. They show emotions such as joy, sorrow, anger, patience, and
4 friendliness. They become excited when they meet old friends.
5 Who are these people? They are not people; they are elephants!
6    Elephants are the largest land animals on Earth. An adult
7 male African elephant can weigh six tons and be 12 feet tall.
8 Females weigh about half as much as males, and are about
9 four feet shorter than males. A newborn elephant, called a
10 calf, weighs about 260 pounds (260 lb) and stands about
11 three feet tall. Elephants usually have two tusks. These are
12 long, pointed teeth that extend from the elephant's mouth. An
13 elephant's tusks grow all through its life, and an elephant
14 may live 60 years or more. The tusks of an old male may
15 reach nine feet in length. Elephants only use their tusks for
16 protection. They do not use them to kill, because elephants

17 are vegetarians; that is, they do not eat any meat. They only
18 eat plants.
19     Elephants are the giants of the animal kingdom, but their
20 size is not their only uncommon feature. The most unusual
21 characteristic of an elephant is its trunk. An elephant uses it
22 to smell, wash, eat, drink, "talk," and hug. However, elephant
23 babies do not know how to use their trunks, just as human
24 babies are not born with the ability to walk. Learning to walk
25 is not easy, and it takes a lot of practice. In the same way
26 baby elephants also learn how to use their trunks well.
27     Over the last 20 years, people have studied elephants and
28 how they live. Consequently, we are beginning to understand
29 these fascinating giant creatures. Unfortunately, their num-
30 bers are quickly decreasing. People are killing elephants to
31 make money by selling their tusks. An elephant's tusks are
32 made of ivory. People use ivory to make bracelets, rings, and
33 other ornaments. Illegal hunters are killing many elephants
34 for their valuable ivory. In 1975, there were about 1.5 million
35 African elephants. Now there are fewer than 600,000. As a
36 result, people are worried that they may become extinct.
37 Some countries are trying to stop the killing of so many ele-
38 phants. They are making laws to protect elephants.
39     Many people travel to Africa to see its beautiful country-
40 side and its unusual animals. In fact, tourism is important to
41 the economy of many African countries. Elephants are a part
42 of the tourist attraction. With cooperation among countries
43 around the world, elephants may continue to live, so that
44 everyone can see these fascinating giants of the Earth.

## A. Fact-Finding Exercise

Read the passage once. Then read the following statements. Check whether
they are true (T) or false (F). If a statement is false, change the statement so
that it is true. Then go back to the passage and find the line that supports
your answer.

  ✗ T      F    1. An elephant's tusks are long, pointed teeth.

  _____ T   ✗ F    2. Female elephants weigh about six tons.

_____ T   ✗ F   3. Elephants eat only meat.

_____

_____ T   ✗ F   4. The number of elephants in Africa is increasing.

_____

✗ T   _____ F   5. Some people kill elephants for their tusks.

_____

## B. Information Recall

Read the passage a second time. Then try to answer the following questions.
Do not look back at the passage. Compare your answers with a classmate's
answers.

*They live with their relative.*

1.   How are elephants similar to people? Please explain your answer.
*They live in a group the family. and they show emotion.*

2.   a.   Describe a full-grown male elephant.
*An adult male elephant can weigh six tons and be 12 feet tall.*

   b.   Describe a full-grown female elephant.
*Females elephant weigh half as much as males, and 4 feet shorter than males.*

   c.   Describe a newborn elephant.
*A newborn elephant can weight about 260 lb and stand 3 feet tall.*

3.   What is the most unusual characteristic of an elephant? What does an
elephant use it for?
*The most unusual characteristic of an elephant is the tru elephant use it to smell, wash, eat, drink, talk" and hug.*

4.   Why do some people kill elephants?
*They kill elephants to make money to sell their tusks.*

## C. Reading Analysis

Read each question carefully. Either circle the letter of the correct answer, or write your answer in the space provided.

1. What is the main idea of this passage?
   a. Elephants, the largest land animals on Earth, are very unusual.
   b. Many people kill elephants for their tusks.
   c. Elephants are very large animals that live in Africa.

2. Elephants show emotions **such as** joy, sorrow, anger, patience, and friendliness.
   a. What are emotions?
      1. ideas
      2. characteristics
      3. feelings
   b. What does **such as** mean?
      1. for example
      2. except
      3. and also

3. An adult male African elephant can weigh six tons. Females weigh about half as much as males.
   How much do females usually weigh?

   _____

4. Elephants usually have two tusks. These are long, pointed teeth that **extend** from the elephant's mouth.
   a. Tusks are
      1. lips
      2. teeth
      3. tongues
   b. The elephant's tusks
      1. are inside the elephant's mouth
      2. are outside the elephant's mouth
   c. **Extend** means
      1. spread out in length
      2. hang down
      3. are heavy

5.  An elephant's tusks grow all through its life, and an elephant may live 60 years or more.
    a.  Can an elephant live to be 65 years old?

        _____ Yes, it can _____

    b.  Do all elephants live to be 60 years old?

        _____ NO. _____

6.  Elephants are vegetarians; **that is**, they do not eat any meat. They only eat plants.
    a.  Vegetarians eat
        1.  meat
        2.  plants
        3.  meat and plants
    b.  **That is** introduces
        1.  an explanation of the word in front of it
        2.  an example of the word in front of it
        3.  an opposite of the word in front of it

7.  Elephants are the giants of the animal kingdom, but their size is not their only **uncommon feature**. The most unusual characteristic of an elephant is its trunk.
    a.  In these sentences, which word is a synonym of **uncommon**?

        _____ unsual _____

    b.  What does **uncommon** mean?
        1.  rare; special
        2.  funny; strange
        3.  ugly; unattractive
    c.  In these sentences, which word is a synonym of **feature**?

        _____ characteristic _____

    d.  What does **feature** mean?
        1.  arm; leg
        2.  quality; trait
        3.  appearance; look

8.  An elephant uses its trunk to smell, wash, eat, drink, "**talk**," and hug.

    Why is the word **talk** in quotation marks (" ")?
    a.  because it is unusual for animals to talk
    b.  because people cannot understand animal speech
    c.  because elephants cannot really talk

9.  Elephant babies do not know how to use their trunks, just as human babies are not born with the ability to walk. As human babies grow, they try to crawl, then to stand, and finally to walk. **In the same way**, baby elephants also learn how to use their trunks well.

    **In the same way** indicates that
    a.   elephant babies and human babies are similar  ╱
    b.   elephant babies and human babies are different

10. **Over the last 20 years**, people have studied elephants and how they live. **Consequently**, we are beginning to understand these fascinating giant creatures. **Unfortunately**, their numbers are quickly decreasing. As a result, people are worried that they may become **extinct**.
    a.   **Over the last 20 years** means
         1.   from 20 years ago until now
         2.   from now until 20 years in the future
         3.   from ten years ago until ten years in the future
    b.   In this paragraph, which word or phrase is a synonym of **consequently**?

         _____

    c.   Complete the following sentence with the appropriate choice.

         Lisa didn't study for her history test. As a result,
         1.   she knew all the answers
         2.   she didn't know any answers  ╱
    d.   **Unfortunately** refers to something
         1.   good
         2.   bad ╱
    e.   Complete the following sentence correctly.

         Eileen wanted to go on a picnic. Unfortunately,
         1.   it began to rain
         2.   the weather was nice
         3.   she invited her friends
    f.   People are worried that elephants may become **extinct**.

         People are worried that
         1.   all the elephants will only be in zoos
         2.   the number of elephants will be very small
         3.   all the elephants will die  ╱

11. Many people travel to Africa to see its beautiful countryside and its unusual animals. In fact, **tourism** is important to the economy of many African countries.

What is **tourism?**
a.  when people travel to different places  ╱
b.  when people see unusual animals
c.  when people work in another country

---

## D. Word Forms

### Part 1

In English, verbs change to nouns in several ways. Some verbs become nouns by adding the suffix *-ion* or *-ation*, for example, *suggest* (v.), *suggestion* (n.). Be careful of spelling changes, for example, *combine* (v.), *combination* (n.).

Complete each sentence with the correct form of the words on the left. **Write all the verbs in the simple present tense. All the verbs are affirmative. The nouns may be singular or plural.**

protect (v.)
protection (n.)

1.  All animal mothers _____ their babies. They give their babies _____ until the babies can take care of themselves.

attract (v.)
attraction (n.)

2.  I want to live in a cool climate. This idea _____ me very much. A cool climate has many _____ for me because I like winter sports.

cooperate (v.)
cooperation (n.)

3.  The government needs the complete _____ of the people to save water this summer. The people usually_____, so there will be enough water for the hot, dry summer months.

*Say one*

fascinate (v.)
fascination (n.)

4.  Effie's_____with wild animals started when she was a child. The unusual animals of Africa and Australia still _____ her today.

continue (v.)
continuation (n.)

5.  An elephant's tusks _____ to grow after it becomes an adult. This _____ of growth is unusual for most animals.

## Part 2

In English, the noun form and the verb form of some words are the same, for example, *cover* (v.), *cover* (n.).

Complete each sentence with the correct form of the word on the left. In addition, indicate whether you are using the verb (v.) or the noun (n.) form of each word. **Write all the verbs in the simple present tense. All the verbs are negative. The nouns may be singular or plural.**

use            1.  A plastic bag has many _____, for exam-
                   (v., n.)
                   ple, carrying books and other items and throwing
                   away garbage. However, people _____
                   (v., n.)
                   them around small children.

practice       2.  Matthew bought a guitar last week, but he
                   _____ because he doesn't have much time.
                   (v., n.)
                   He will need a lot of _____ , however,
                   (v., n.)
                   before he can play well.

walk           3.  Barbara likes to take long _____ in the
                   (v., n.)
                   park when the weather is warm. However, she
                   _____ in the park at all during the winter
                   (v., n.)
                   because she doesn't like cold weather.

decrease       4.  The number of wild animals in a country
                   _____ if the animals and their environment
                   (v., n.)
                   are protected. The destruction of forests and jungles
                   in some places is causing the large _____ in
                   (v., n.)
                   the number of some wild animals.

value          5.  Silver and gold have a very high _____ all
                   (v., n.)
                   over the world. However, most people _____
                   (v., n.)
                   copper very highly, and it is not as expensive as
                   gold or silver.

# E. Vocabulary in Context

ability (n.) Tài năng/khả ~~fascinating (adj.)~~ làm mê    protect (v.) bảo vệ, che chở
as a result Kết quả như    features (n.) đặc điểm    unusual (adj.) Kỳ lạ, bất thường
cooperation (n.) liên    heads (n.) đầu, chóp    unfortunately (adj.) Rủi không may
extinct (adj.) mất, qua rồi

Read each sentence below. Fill in each space with the correct word from the list above. Use each word only once.

1. Parents always _____ their children from getting hurt.

2. Many animals on exhibition in museums are _____, for example, all dinosaurs.

3. My new car has several extra _____: air conditioning, a radio, and a cassette player.

4. Kings, emperors, and presidents are _____ of their countries.

5. Roberta needed the help and _____ of her friends last week because she moved to a new apartment. She was not able to move by herself.

6. Snow in July is _____. It almost never happens.

7. Many people believe that travel to other planets will be possible in the 21st century. This is a(n) _____ idea!

8. Michael wanted to go to the movies last night. _____, he had a lot of homework to do, so he stayed home.

9. Allen studied very hard for his English exam. _____, the test was easy for him, and he did very well.

10. Susan has the _____ to learn other languages very quickly.

## F. Follow-up Activities

1. Work with a partner. Make a list of five places and the reasons for visiting them.
2. Choose a place you want to visit. Go to a travel agency and get brochures (booklets) for this place. Read the information, and report to your class on the country. Give reasons why you want to visit this place.
3. Alone, or with a classmate from your country, prepare a travel brochure for your country, and describe why you think people will be interested in visiting it.
4. The United States measures height in feet and inches. The United States measures weight in pounds and tons. However, most countries do not measure height in feet. They do not measure weight in pounds and tons. Instead, they use the metric system. They measure height in meters, and weight in kilograms and metric tons. Use the following chart to answer the questions.

## U.S. TO METRIC CONVERSION

**WEIGHT**

1 Ton = 2000 Pounds
1 Ton = .907 Metric Ton
1 Pound (lb) = .45 Kilogram (kg)

**HEIGHT**

1 Foot (ft) = .30 meter (m)
1 Inch (in) = 2.54 centimeters (cm)

a. How much does an adult female elephant weigh in tons?

_____

b. How many metric tons does an adult female elephant weigh?
   ① 2.7 metric tons
   2. 5 metric tons
   3. 1.1 metric tons

c. How much does an elephant baby weigh in pounds?

_____

d. How much does an elephant baby weigh in kilograms?
   1. 207 kilos
   2. 301 kilos
   ③ 117 kilos

e. How tall is an adult male elephant in feet?

_____

f. How tall is an adult male elephant in meters?
  1. 8.1 meters
  ②. 3.6 meters
  3. 1.6 meters

g. How tall is an elephant baby in feet?

_____

h. How tall is an elephant baby in meters?
  1. 3.1 meters
  2. 0.9 meters
  3. 2.2 meters

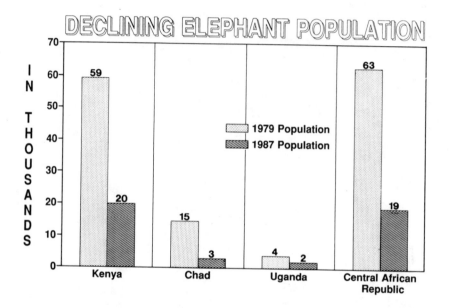

5. Refer to the chart. Write the answers to the following questions.
  a. Which country had the most elephants in 1979?

_____

  b. Which country had the most elephants in 1987?

_____

  c. In which country did the largest number of elephants die?

_____

  d. What does **declining** mean?
    1. increasing
    ②. decreasing
    3. changing

## G. Topics for Discussion and Writing

1.  Elephants are very social animals. Do you know of any other animal that is social, too? Describe it.
2.  Do you think it is right for people to kill elephants for their tusks? Why, or why not? State your opinion. Give reasons and examples.
3.  Are there sometimes good reasons to kill animals? What are these reasons? What are some bad reasons to kill animals? Work with a partner. Make a chart. List good and bad reasons. Compare your chart with your other classmates' charts.

## H. Crossword Puzzle: Elephants

**Across Clues**

1. The continent where many elephants live
7. Joy, sorrow, and anger are _emotion_ .
8. One unusual _feature_ of an elephant is its long nose.
11. The largest land animal _elephant_
13. Bracelets, rings, and earrings are kinds of _ornaments_.
14. The opposite of **in**
15. Elephants are very interesting. They are very _fascinating_ .
18. An elephant's large teeth are made of _ivory_ .
19. Many people kill elephants for _money_ .
20. The opposite of **yes**   _NO_
21. The opposite of **bottom**   _Top_
22. An elephant's _Tusk_ are two long teeth that come out of its mouth.
24. The opposite of **no**   _yes_

**Down Clues**

2. When countries work together, they _cooperate_ with each other.
3. I like ice cream, _but_ John does not.
4. An elephant is _not_ small. It is very big.
5. The opposite of **on**   _off_
6. An elephant's nose is called a _Trunk_ .
7. When there are no more elephants, they will be _extinct_ .
9. As a result
10. A person who does not eat meat is a _vegetarian_ .
12. Baby elephants need to _practice_ using their long noses.
15. The opposite of **remember**   _Forget_
16. Two, four, six, eight, _Ten_
17. Elephants are very large. In fact, they are _giant_ .
23. The opposite of **down**   _up._

## I. CLOZE Quiz

| | | |
|---|---|---|
| be | have | stand |
| eat | live | use |
| grow | reach | weigh |

Read the passage below. Fill in each space with one of the verbs listed above. Use the simple present tense in either the affirmative or the negative. You may use the words more than once.

Elephants (1) ___*are*___ the largest land animals on earth. An adult male African elephant (2) ___*weigh*___ six tons and (3) ___*be*___ 12 feet tall. Females (4) ___*weigh*___ about half as much as males, and (5) ___*stand*___ about four feet shorter than males. A newborn elephant, called a calf, (6) ___*weighs*___ about 260 lb and (7) ___*stands*___ about three feet tall. Elephants usually (8) ___*have*___ two tusks. An elephant's tusks (9) ___*grow*___ all through its life, and an elephant (10) ___*lives*___ 60 years or more. The tusks of an old male (11) ___*reach*___ nine feet in length. However, elephants only (12) ___*use*___ their tusks for protection. They (13) ___*do not use*___ them to kill, because elephants are vegetarians; that is, they (14) ___*do not eat*___ any meat. They only (15) ___*eat*___ plants.

# CHAPTER 2

# The Extinction of the Dinosaurs: What Happened?

*extinct (adj)*
*qua toi, mat*

## Prereading Preparation

1. Look at the photograph on the left. What is this a picture of? Where is this?
2. Are dinosaurs alive today?
3. When did dinosaurs live? What did they eat?
4. What happened to them?   *happen(v) xảy ra, tình cờ*
5. How do you think they became extinct?

*incredible : không thể tưởng tượng được*

1 From the time most people are children, they have a fasci-
2 nation with dinosaurs, the largest land animals that ever lived.
3 People young and old visit museums to learn about these
4 giant creatures from the past. As they walk by the huge skele-
5 tons, footprints in stone, and ancient eggs, they wonder what
6 happened to these incredible animals. Why did dinosaurs
7 become extinct?   *2 tự tuyệt dc*
8 Scientists had many theories to explain the dinosaur
9 extinction. They said that the climate of the Earth slowly
10 changed. As it gradually became colder, plants died. Some
11 dinosaurs were vegetarians, so they died, too. Another theory
12 is that dinosaurs simply became too big to live. After all, some
13 dinosaurs weighed as much as 77 tons. A third theory is that
14 some small animals ate the dinosaurs' eggs. However, many
15 other species of plants and animals also died out at the same
16 time as the dinosaurs. People were still uncertain because
17 none of the theories explained these extinctions.

*fascinate (v) thu hút, hấp dẫn*
*creature : tạo vật*
*creature · being*
*huge · giant*
*skeleton : bộ xương*
*ancient : old*
*extinct : mất, qua r*
*theories : lý thu*
*explain(v) giải thích*

18    Then, in the 1980s, scientists began to discuss a new
19    theory. Their theory is that 65 million years ago, a large comet
20    or asteroid struck the Earth near Mexico. It struck at incredi-
21    bly high speed—as high as 15,000 miles per hour. It was very
22    damaging. In fact, it created a hole 25 miles deep and 100
23    miles in diameter. The dirt and ash blew high up into the sky.
24    They covered the entire planet with a thin layer of dust, which
25    blocked the sun for many months. The temperature decreased
26    significantly all around the Earth for a long time, perhaps
27    years. Plants died rapidly because there was not enough sun-
28    light. Animals also died quickly because they had nothing to
29    eat and because the climate was too cold.
30    Right now, this new theory explains the extinction of many
31    kinds of life 65 million years ago. However, scientists need to
32    find the exact place where the asteroid or comet struck the
33    Earth. When they find the location, they will be able to prove
34    that their theory is correct.

## A. Fact-Finding Exercise

Read the passage once. Then read the following statements. Check whether they are true (T) or false (F). If a statement is false, change the statement so that it is true. Then go back to the passage and find the line that supports your answer.

__X__ T  ____ F  1. Dinosaurs were the largest land animals on Earth.

_We can see the huge skeletons, footprints and aciant egg_

__X__ T  ____ F  2. There are many different theories about the dinosaur extinction.

_____

____ T  __X__ F  3. All dinosaurs were vegetarians.

_____

__X__ T  ____ F  4. Some scientists think a large comet or asteroid struck the Earth 65 million years ago.

_____

____ T  ____ F  5. The comet or asteroid's dirt increased the Earth's temperature.

_____

____ T  __X__ F  6. Scientists know exactly where the comet struck.

_____

## B. Information Recall

Read the passage a second time. Then try to answer the following questions. Do not look back at the passage. Compare your answers with a classmate's answers.

1.  a.  Why do some people visit museums?

_Some people visit museums because they has fascination with dinosaurs, the largest land animal that ever lived_

   b.  What can you see in museums?

_I can see in museums as the huge skeleton, footprints in stone, and acient eggs_

2.  a.  How many theories about dinosaurs are in the second paragraph of the passage?

> *it has many theories about dinosaurs ( three theories )*

   b.  Why do scientists think some vegetarian dinosaurs died?

> *Earth slowly changed. As it gradually became colder,*
> *plants died. Some dinosaurs were vegetarians, so they died too.*

   c.  Were people certain about all these old theories? Why, or why not?

> *people weren't certain about all these theories. because*
> *have a new theory.*

3.  a.  When did scientists discuss a new theory?

> *1980*

   b.  Where did they think the comet or asteroid struck the Earth?

> *Near Mexico*

   c.  How big was the hole in the Earth?

> *25 miles*

   d.  What happened to the Earth's temperature afterward?

> *a large Comet and asteroid struck the Earth near Mexico*

   e.  Why did the plants and animals die?

> *the dirt and ask blew → climate was too cold.*

4.  How can scientists prove this new theory?

> *Scientists need to find exact place where the steroid*
> *and comet struck the earth*

---

## C. Reading Analysis

Read each question carefully. Either circle the letter of the correct answer, or write your answer in the space provided.

1.  What is the main idea of this passage?
    a.  The asteroid or comet created a hole 25 miles deep and 100 miles in diameter.
    b.  Dinosaurs were the largest animals that ever lived on Earth.
    c.  Scientists have a new theory to explain how dinosaurs became extinct.

2.  Dinosaurs are the **largest** land animals that ever lived. **People young and old** visit museums to learn about these giant **creatures** from the past.

 a.  In these sentences, which word is a synonym of **large**?

 _____ *giant* _____

 b.  **People young and old** means
   1.  young people
   2.  old people
   3.  people of any age
   4.  young people or old people  ✓

 c.  In these sentences, which word is a synonym for **creatures**?

 _____ *animal* _____

3.  People **wonder** what happened to these incredible animals. **Why did dinosaurs become extinct?**

 a.  The word **wonder** means
   1.  know
   2.  think about  ✓
   3.  ask

 b.  The question **Why did dinosaurs become extinct?** means
   1.  Why did all the dinosaurs die?  ✓
   2.  Why are dinosaurs in museums?
   3.  Why were dinosaurs so big?

4.  Scientists had many **theories** to explain the dinosaur extinction. They said that the **climate** of the Earth slowly changed. Some dinosaurs were **vegetarians**. As it **gradually** became colder, plants died, so the animals that were vegetarians died, too.

 a.  Theories are
   1.  scientific ideas  ✓
   2.  extinctions
   3.  scientific examples

 b.  **Climate** refers to the Earth's
   1.  land
   2.  oceans
   3.  weather  ✓

 c.  Why did the vegetarian dinosaurs die?
   1.  It was too cold.
   2.  There were no plants to eat.  ✓
   3.  The Earth changed.

 d.  In these sentences, which word is a synonym of **gradually**?

 _____ *slowly.* _____

5.  One theory is that dinosaurs simply became too big to live. **After all**, some dinosaurs weighed as much as 77 tons.

    The information that follows **after all**
    a.  gives details to support the sentence before it  ⟋
    b.  gives new information about another idea
    c.  gives some kind of numbers

6.  People were still **uncertain** because **none of** the theories explained these extinctions.
    a.  **Uncertain** means
        1.  not alive
        2.  not sure ⟍
        3.  confused
    b.  **None of** means
        1.  one
        2.  zero  ⟋
        3.  all

7.  The new theory is that 65 million years ago, a large comet or asteroid struck the Earth at incredibly high speed—as high as 15,000 miles per hour. It was very damaging. **In fact**, it created a hole 25 miles deep and 100 miles in **diameter**.
    a.  What follows the dash (—)?
        1.  an example
        2.  a contrast  ⟍
        3.  an explanation
    b.  What is the purpose of **in fact**?
        1.  It gives true information. ⟋
        2.  It introduces details to support information.
        3.  It introduces different information.
    c.  **Diameter** describes
        1.  height
        2.  width  ⟋  bề rộ, ngang
        3.  depth

8.  The temperature **decreased** all around the Earth for a long time, perhaps years. Plants died **rapidly** because there was **not enough** sunlight. Animals also died quickly because they had nothing to eat and because weather the climate was too cold.
    a.  **Decreased** means
        1.  became higher
        2.  became lower  ⟍

create (ʋ) Two ta.

   b.  In these sentences, which word is a synonym of **rapidly**?

                     *quickly*

   c.  **Not enough** means
      1.  too little ✓
      2.  too much

9.  The new theory explains the extinction of many kinds of life 65 million years ago. **However,** scientists need to find the **exact** place where the asteroid or comet struck the Earth. When they find the **location,** they will be able to prove that their theory is **correct.**

   a.  **However** means
      1.  and
      2.  so
      3.  but ✓

   b.  What does **exact** mean?
      1.  specific
      2.  best ✓
      3.  damaged   *làm hại, tổn thương*

   c.  In these sentences, which word is a synonym of **location**?

                     *place*

   d.  **Correct** means
      1.  extinct
      2.  comet
      3.  true ✓

## D. Word Forms

### Part 1

In English, many adjectives change to adverbs by adding the suffix -*ly*, for example, *simple* (adj.), *simply* (adv.). If the adjective ends in -*e*, drop the -*e* before adding -*ly*, for example, *reasonable* (adj.), *reasonably* (adv.).

Complete each sentence with the correct form of the words on the left.

exact (adj.)

exactly (adv.)

1. I asked Patricia for the _____ location of the movie theater. I need to know _____ where it is because I am going to meet my friends there.

incredible (adj.)

incredibly (adv.)

2. Irene works _____ hard. She does an _____ amount of work every day. She needs to relax more.

significant (adj.)

significantly (adv.)

3. When Eugene got a higher position in his company, he also got a _____ pay raise. Because his income increased _____, he was able to buy a house.

rapid (adj.)

rapidly (adv.)

4. Some people believe that a _____ change in the weather makes them catch colds. However, even when the weather _____ becomes cold and wet, it does not make people sick.

gradual (adj.)

gradually (adv.)

5. Carol plays tennis every week. She is noticing a _____ improvement in her game. As she _____ gets better, more people want to play tennis with her.

*ad verb*

## Part 2

In English, the noun form and the verb form of some words are the same, for example, *help* (v.), *help* (n.).

Complete each sentence with the correct form of the word on the left. In addition, indicate whether you are using the verb (v.) or the noun (n.) form of each word. **Write all the verbs in the simple past tense. They may be affirmative or negative. The nouns may be singular or plural.**

change  1.  Harry wrote an interesting story, but then he made many

_changes_ in it. He actually _changed_ it so much that
(v., n.)                          (v., n.)

he gave it a different title.

visit  2.  Doris always _visited_ her grandparents on their birth-
(v., n.)

days. These _visits_ were special for her, and she
(v., n.)

remembers them well.

damage  3.  The fire at the car dealership caused a lot of _damage_.
(v., n.)

It _damaged_ the showroom, the repair shop, and several
(v., n.)

cars in the parking lot, too.

cover  4.  Betty forgot to put a heavy _cover_ on the pot of
(v., n.)

tomato sauce. She _didn't cover_ the pot, so the sauce
(v., n.)

boiled over onto the stove.

decrease  5.  After Gino's Restaurant got a new cook, the number

of customers _decreased_ significantly. The new cook
(v., n.)

was terrible — he caused the unfortunate _decrease_
(v., n.)

in business.

---

# E. Vocabulary in Context

| | | |
|---|---|---|
| climate (n.) | in fact | simply (adv.) |
| creature (n.) | incredibly (adv.) | theory (n.) |
| discuss (v.) | prove (v.) | uncertain (adj.) |
| giant (adj.) | | |

Read each sentence below. Fill in each space with the correct word from the list above. Use each word only once.

1. Joann plans to come into town today, but I am ___uncertain___ whether her train arrives at 4 P.M. or at 5 P.M.

2. One dinosaur, the Brachiosaurus, was 74 feet long and weighed 77 tons. It certainly was a ___giant___ animal!

3. Some scientists believe that they have found a new planet. However, it will take time before they can ___prove___ their idea.

4. Diplodocus was a vegetarian dinosaur. This ancient ___creature___ was 88 feet long.

5. During the dinosaur age, the Earth's ___climate___ was very warm, even in areas that are very cold today.

6. Many scientists agree with the ___theory___ that dinosaurs were very social animals, but they need more evidence to support their idea.

7. Some dinosaurs, such as Compsognathus, were very small. ___In fact___ , this dinosaur was only 28 inches long.

8. Margaret and Andrés need a new car. They will probably ___discuss___ the type of car they need before they buy one.

9. The hottest place on Earth has a temperature of 135° F, but the planet Venus is ___incredibly___ hot: 890° F!

10. It is very easy to cook eggs. You ___simply___ put them in boiling water for three minutes.

## F. Follow-up Activities

1. Work with a classmate from your country. Make a list of the most famous museums in your country. Tell your other classmates about your country's museums.

2. Did you visit any museums in this country? Tell your classmates about them.

3. a. Find out about interesting museums in this city.
   b. Call these museums and find out their locations.
   c. Then fill in the following chart.

| Museum | Location | Hours | Admission Fee | Contents |
|--------|----------|-------|---------------|----------|
| _____ | _____ | _____ | _____ | _____ |
| _____ | _____ | _____ | _____ | _____ |
| _____ | _____ | _____ | _____ | _____ |

   d. Choose one museum to visit with your classmates. Report to the class about the most interesting exhibit there.

## G. Topics for Discussion and Writing

1. Do you think it is important to know what happened to dinosaurs? Why, or why not?
2. It is possible for a large comet or asteroid to strike the Earth again. If it does, what do you think will happen? Work with a classmate to make a list of things that will happen. Compare your list with your classmates' lists.
3. Imagine that an asteroid has just struck the Earth. Describe what you see, hear, and feel.

# H. Crossword Puzzle: The Extinction of the Dinosaurs

**Across Clues**

2. I ____AM____ ; you are.
6. __DINOSAURS__ were the largest land animals on Earth.
7. The opposite of **yes**   NO
8. I see you. You see ____ME____ .
10. The past tense of **do**   did
12. Animals
13. Kinds of animals that do not exist any more are __extinct__ .
14. We talk about the __CLIMATE__ when we describe the weather in general.
16. A __THEORY__ is an idea that has no proof.
20. When you have evidence to show that something is true, you can __PROVE__ it.
21. Become less   DECREASE
22. Noticeably   SIGNIFICANTLY
24. Place   LOCATION
25. 2,000 pounds equals one __TON__ .

**Down Clues**

1. Plants need __SUNLIGHT__ in order to live.
2. A large object in outer space   ASTEROID
3. Very large   GIANT
4. I am; he ____IS____ .
5. Slowly; over a long time   GRADUALLY
8. A __MUSEUM__ is a building where you can see objects from the past and from other cultures.
9. The speed limit on the highway is 55 miles __PER__ hour.
11. The __DIAMETER__ of a circle shows how wide the circle is.
15. An animal that does not eat meat is a __VEGETARIAN__
17. The past tense of **eat**   ATE
18. __MEXICO__ is the country where people think the asteroid struck the Earth.
19. The opposite of **down**   UP
23. The opposite of **no**   YES

## I. CLOZE Quiz

| | | |
|---|---|---|
| be | cover | die |
| begin | create | have |
| block | decrease | strike |
| blow | | |

Read the passage below. Fill in each space with the simple past tense of one of the verbs listed above. You may use the words more than once.

In the 1980s, scientists (1) _____began_____ to discuss a new theory. Their theory is that 65 million years ago, a large comet or asteroid (2) _____struck_____ the Earth near Mexico. It (3) _____struck_____ at incredibly high speed—as high as 15,000 miles per hour. It (4) _____was_____ very damaging. In fact, it (5) _____created_____ a hole 25 miles deep and 100 miles in diameter. The dirt and ash (6) _____blew_____ high up into the sky. They (7) _____covered_____ the entire planet with a thin layer of dust, which (8) _____blocked_____ the sun for many months. The temperature (9) _____decreased_____ significantly all around the Earth for a long time, perhaps years. Plants (10) _____died_____ rapidly because there (11) _____was_____ not enough sunlight. Animals also (12) _____died_____ quickly because they (13) _____had_____ nothing to eat and because the climate (14) _____was_____ too cold.

## Unit I Discussion

What are some similarities between elephants and dinosaurs? For example, what physical characteristics and habits do they have in common?

# UNIT II

## A Taste of America
culture

# CHAPTER 3
# The All-American Diner

---

## Prereading Preparation

1. Look at the photograph on the left. What is this a picture of? What kind of food can you eat there? Is the food expensive?
2. Do you go out to eat? Where do you go? What kind of restaurant do you eat in? What kinds of food do you like to eat when you eat out? Are these places expensive? Is the service fast?
3. Think of some places to eat in this city. Make a chart with information about them.

| Name of Restaurant | Type of Food | Cost (expensive, moderate, cheap) |
|---|---|---|
| Mc Donald's | Hamberger | cheap. |
| VINH LONG | CHINESE Food | cheap |
| Burgger King. | Hampbuger | cheap. |
|  |  |  |
|  |  |  |

4. What are some all-American activities?
5. Why are diners all-American?

6. Following is a list of people. With a partner, write which workers people usually give tips to, and how much they usually tip.

| Yes/No | How Much | People |
|--------|----------|--------|
| ___/___ | _____ | taxi driver   *Yes* |
| _____ | _____ | cashier in a supermarket   *No* |
| _____ | _____ | waiter or waitress |
| _____ | _____ | teacher   *N* |
| _____ | _____ | porter in a hotel or train station   *yes* |
| _____ | _____ | police officer   *No* |
| _____ | _____ | gas station attendant |
| _____ | _____ | newspaper carrier |
| _____ | _____ | salesperson in a department store   *no* |
| _____ | _____ | beautician or barber |

1  Do you like to eat out? Do you like to eat quickly? Do you
2  like inexpensive food? Some people go to fast-food restaurants
3  for these reasons. In the past, people usually went to diners
4  for these reasons. In fact, many people still go to diners today
5  for the same reasons.
6  A man named Walter Scott had the first "diner" in 1872. It
7  wasn't really a diner. It was only a simple food cart. People on
8  the street walked up to the cart to buy food. These carts served
9  late-night workers who wanted a cup of coffee and a late-night
10  meal. The meal was a sandwich or boiled eggs. In 1887,
11  Samuel Messer Jones built the first diner big enough to allow
12  the customers to come inside. However, they did not sit down.
13  Later, people built diners with counters and stools, and people
14  sat down while they ate.
15  Before long, many diners stayed open around the clock. In
16  other words, people were able to eat in a diner at any time.
17  Diners changed in other ways, too. The original menu of sand-
18  wiches and coffee became bigger. It included soup, favorite
19  dishes, and a breakfast menu. In addition, diners soon became
20  permanent buildings. They were no longer carts on wheels.
21  Diners today look similar to the diners of the early 1900s. They
22  are usually rectangular buildings with large windows. Inside, the
23  diners have shining counters with stools, booths, and tables and
24  chairs. People can eat all three meals in a modern diner.

25     Today, many people eat in fast-food restaurants such as
26  McDonald's and Burger King. However, the diner remains an
27  American tradition, and thousands of people still enjoy eating
28  there. It was popular a century ago, and it is still popular today.

## A. Fact-Finding Exercise

Read the passage once. Then read the following statements. Check whether they are true (T) or false (F). If a statement is false, change the statement so that it is true. Then go back to the passage and find the line that supports your answer.

___✓ T  ___ F   1. Diners existed before fast-food restaurants existed.

___ T  ___✗ F   2. Diners began as permanent buildings.
              *they began as simple food carts*

___✓ T  ___ F   3. The first diners served people who worked late.

___ T  ___✓ F   4. In 1887, Samuel Messer Jones built the first diner for people to sit in.
              *He built the first diner big enough for people to come in*

___ T  ___✓ F   5. The original diner menu never changed.
              *The original menu became bigger*

___✓ T  ___ F   6. Diners are still popular today.

## B. Information Recall

Read the passage a second time. Then try to answer the following questions. Do not look back at the passage. Compare your answers with a classmate's answers.

1.  a.  How did diners begin?
      *They began a simple food carts*
      *late-night works ate there*

    b.  Who ate at the first diners?
      *The menu became bigger. They included more foods*
      *they included all three meals*

2.  How did the menus change over the years?

    *The menu became bigger. They included more foods.*
    *they included all three meals*
    *with .... were available.*

3.  How do most diners look from the outside? How do they look on the inside?

    *From the outside, they are usually rectangular buildings*
    *with large windows. On the inside, they have counters*
    *with stools, booths and tables*

4.  How did diners change from 1872 to today?

    _____

    _____

5.  Put the following sentences in the correct order.

    _4_  1. Samuel Messer Jones built the first diner big enough for people to come inside.

    _3_  2. Diners became big enough for people to sit in.

    _1_  3. Diners served only late-night meals.

    _2_  4. Diners began as food carts.

    _5_  5. Diners were open around the clock.

---

## C. Reading Analysis

Read each question carefully. Either circle the letter of the correct answer, or write your answer in the space provided.

1.  What is the main idea of this passage?
    a.  The diner is a traditional, popular place to eat in the United States.
    b.  Samuel Messer Jones built the first diner big enough to allow the customers to come inside.
    c.  American diners serve many types of food 24 hours a day to their customers.

2.  A man named Walter Scott had the first **"diner"** in 1872. People on the street walked up to the cart to buy food.

    Why is **diner** in quotation marks?
    a.  because it is spelled differently from **dinner**
    b.  because the first diner was not a real diner
    c.  because **diner** was a new word

3.  The first diners served late-night workers who wanted a cup of coffee and a late-night **meal**. The meal was a sandwich or boiled eggs. Before long, the original menu of sandwiches and coffee became bigger. It included soup, favorite dishes, and a breakfast menu. People can eat all three meals in a modern diner.

    a.  How many meals did the first diners serve?
        1.  only one
        2.  two
        3.  all three
    b.  Today, which meals do diners serve?
        1.  only breakfast
        2.  only lunch
        3.  only dinner
        4.  all three meals
    c.  What does **meal** mean?
        1.  the food a person eats with coffee
        2.  the food a person eats at one time
        3.  the food a person eats at a table

4.  Diners stayed open **around the clock**. *against* **In other words**, people were able to eat in a diner at any time.

    a.  **Around the clock** means
        1.  12 hours a day
        2.  24 hours a day
    b.  What follows **in other words**?
        1.  new information about the idea before it     *restatement (u)*
        2.  a restatement of the idea before it          *Trình bày trở*
        3.  opposite information about the idea before it

5.  The original menu of sandwiches and coffee became bigger. **It** included soup, favorite dishes, and a breakfast menu. **In addition**, diners soon became permanent buildings. They were no longer carts on wheels.

    a.  What does **it** refer to?
        1.  menu
        2.  coffee
        3.  soup
    b.  According to this paragraph, diners changed in
        1.  two ways
        2.  three ways
        3.  four ways

c.   What are the ways that diners changed?

_sandwiches and coffee became bigger. It included soup_
_favorite, dishes and a breakfast menu, in addition_
_diners from became permanent buildings._

d.   What does **in addition** mean?
1.   but
2.   so
3.   and ⁄

e.   Complete the following sentence with the appropriate choice.

Steven bought fruit and vegetables. In addition,
1.   he went to the post office to mail a letter
2.   he bought milk, chicken, and bread  ⁓
3.   he called his friend and invited him to dinner.

6.   Today, many people eat in fast-food restaurants **such as** McDonald's and Burger King.
a.   What does **such as** mean?
1.   in addition
2.   for example ⁄
3.   but

b.   What are McDonald's and Burger King?

_they are fast food restaurant_

c.   Complete the following sentence correctly.

Elizabeth went to the vegetable store. She bought many vegetables, such as
1.   oranges, apples, and bananas
2.   carrots, peas, and broccoli  ⁓
3.   pepper, salt, and oregano

## D. Word Forms

In English, adjectives usually change to adverbs by adding the suffix -*ly*, for example, *sad* (adj.), *sadly* (adv.). If the adjective ends in -*e*, drop the -*e* before adding -*ly*, for example, *reasonable* (adj.), *reasonably* (adv.).

Complete each sentence with the correct form of the words on the left.

quick (adj.)

quickly (adv.)

1. Christopher worked _quickly_ to finish painting his living room before 9 P.M. He was so _quick_ that he finished at 8:30 P.M.

original (adj.)

originally (adv.)

2. The _original_ cars were very simple. They didn't have lights, windows, heat, or a radio. They _originally_ had two seats, an engine, and four wheels.

*resident*

permanent (adj.)

permanently (adv.)

3. Maria came to the United States to make it her _permanent_ home. She wants to live in the United States _permantly_. She will not return to her country.

simple (adj.)

simply (adv.)

4. Alice has a very _simple_ job. She doesn't have many things to do. She _simply_ answers the telephone and types letters.

usual (adj.)

usually (adv.)

5. David's _usual_ dinner time is 7 P.M. In fact, he doesn't _usually_ eat dinner later than 7:30 P.M.

---

## E. Vocabulary in Context

allow (v.)    however (adv.)    popular (adj.)
customer (n.)    in addition    service (n.)
enough (adj.)    include (v.)

Read each sentence below. Fill in each space with the correct word from the list above. Use each word only once.

1.  Louise likes to go to the beach to sit in the sun. _In addition_, she likes to swim and look at the ocean.

2.  Mark is a very _popular_ singer. Millions of people listen to his music and buy his recordings.

3.  The price of this car does not _include_ air conditioning. Air conditioning is $500 extra.

4.  The waiters at the Metropolitan Restaurant like Paul because he is a good _customer_. He always gives big tips.

5.  The Metropolitan Restaurant has very good _service_. The waiters are helpful and polite, and they bring your meal quickly.

6.  I want to buy a new camera, but it costs $150. I only have $100. I do not have _enough_ money.

7.  Marsha does not _allow_ her children to go outside after dark. They have to come inside when the sun goes down.

8.  Elizabeth likes to go to the beach to sit in the sun. _however_, she does not like to swim in the ocean because the water is very cold.

## F. Follow-up Activities

1.  Look at the photograph of the inside of a diner. Label the counter, the
    stools, and the booths.

    a.  If you are with four other people, and you want to have dinner
        together, where is the best place to sit?

        _____ *at the table with chairs* _____

    b.  If you want to stop in a diner alone for a cup of coffee, and you are
        in a hurry, where is the best place to sit?

        _____ *at the counter on a stools.* _____

    c.  If you are with three friends, and you want to sit close together,
        where is the best place to sit?

        _____ *in a booth* _____

# MENU

## Salads
Mixed Green . . . . . . . . . . . . . . . . . . . . . . . . . . 2.75
Tuna . . . . . . . . . . . . . . . . . . . . . . . . . . . . . 4.75
Fresh Fruit . . . . . . . . . . . . . . . . . . . . . . . . . 3.50
      with Cottage Cheese . . . . . . . . . . . . . 4.25

## Soups
Chicken . . . . . . . . . . . . . . . . . . . . . . . . . . . 2.00
Vegetable . . . . . . . . . . . . . . . . . . . . . . . . . . 2.25
Chili . . . . . . . . . . . . . . . . . . . . . . . . . . . . . 3.25

## Sandwiches (Hot & Cold)
Hamburger . . . . . . . . . . . . . . . . . . . . . . . . . 2.75
  Deluxe (w/French fries, lettuce & tomato) . . . 3.75
Cheeseburger . . . . . . . . . . . . . . . . . . . . . . . . 3.35
  Deluxe (w/French fries, lettuce & tomato) . . . 4.35
Bacon, Lettuce, & Tomato . . . . . . . . . . . . . . . 3.25
American Cheese . . . . . . . . . . . . . . . . . . . . . 2.45
Swiss Cheese . . . . . . . . . . . . . . . . . . . . . . . . 2.65
Turkey . . . . . . . . . . . . . . . . . . . . . . . . . . . . 3.65

## Entrees
Roast Beef . . . . . . . . . . . . . . . . . . . . . . . . . 7.00
Fish . . . . . . . . . . . . . . . . . . . . . . . . . . . . . . 6.75
1/2 Chicken (Broiled or Fried) . . . . . . . . . . . . . 4.75
Meat Loaf . . . . . . . . . . . . . . . . . . . . . . . . . . 4.50
     all entrees served with choice of potato and vegetable

## Desserts
Jello . . . . . . . . . . . . . . . . . . . . . . . . . . . . . . 1.50
Ice Cream (different flavors daily) . . . . . . . . . . 1.75
Pies (Apple, Peach, or Blueberry) . . . . . . . . . . 2.25

## Beverages
Coffee . . . . . . . . . . . . . . . . . . . . . . . . . . . . . .75
Tea . . . . . . . . . . . . . . . . . . . . . . . . . . . . . . . .75
Coke, 7-Up, Tab . . . . . . . . . . . . . . . . . . . . . . 1.00

\* Local Sales Tax of 5% on all Checks

2.  Form a group of three or four students. Use the menu to role play a restaurant scene together. One student will play the role of waiter or waitress, and the others will play the roles of customers in a diner. The "waiter" or "waitress" will take orders. The "customers" will order meals. Then the "waiter" or "waitress" will give the "customers" a bill. The "customers" will check the bill, calculate the tax, and figure out a proper tip.

3. a. After the role play, discuss the vocabulary you needed. Write down the important words and phrases you will need when you go to a diner for a meal.
   b. Go to a diner in pairs or groups of three or four. Order a meal. Report to the class. Tell five new vocabulary words or phrases that you learned from your diner experience.

4. Make a list of different kinds of restaurants. Then find out which type of restaurant each classmate likes best.

| **Classmate** | **Favorite Type of Restaurant** |
| --- | --- |
| _____ | _____ |
| _____ | _____ |
| _____ | _____ |
| _____ | _____ |
| _____ | _____ |
| _____ | _____ |
| _____ | _____ |
| _____ | _____ |

## G. Topics for Discussion and Writing

1. Every culture has many traditions about food. Describe a special custom in your country, for example, a wedding or a funeral. Explain how food is an important part of that custom, and what kind of food is prepared.
2. Americans enjoy eating out often. Do you eat out often? Why, or why not? If you do, where do you go and what do you eat? If you don't, what do you eat at home?
3. In the United States, when people eat out, they sometimes treat other people. In other words, one person pays for everyone else's meal. When do you think people treat other people in the United States? When do you treat people in your country? Compare your answers with your classmates' answers.
4. In the United States, when people eat out, they sometimes go "Dutch treat." This means that each person pays for his or her own meal. Think of a situation where people go Dutch treat in the United States. Do people ever go Dutch treat in your country? When? If they don't, why not? Compare your answers with your classmates' answers.

# H. Crossword Puzzle: The All-American Diner

## Across Clues

1. A synonym of **but** however
4. I was hungry. They _____ were _____ hungry.
6. Three hot drinks are tea, _____ coffee _____, and hot chocolate.
8. The opposite of **no** yes
11. 2 plus 2 is _____ not _____ 5. It is 4.
12. Lunch and dinner are two of the three _____ meals _____ we eat each day.
14. The opposite of **small** , big
15. The first diners were able to move because they had four _____ wheels _____ .
16. Diners changed from carts on wheels to _____ permanent _____ buildings.
19. People sometimes eat cereal or eggs and toast for _____ breakfast _____ .

## Down Clues

1. _____ is a short way to say hello.
2. Diners originally served late-night _____ who wanted something to eat.
3. The food in most diners is _____ good. Everyone likes it!
5. Diners are not round or square. They are _____ .
7. The opposite of **slow**
9. I _____ hungry. We are hungry.
10. Apples are my _____ fruit. I like apples better than any other fruit.
13. Burger King is a fast-food _____ .

20. _____ diner serves food quickly. In other words, *all* diners serve food quickly.
21. In a diner, you can sit on a chair at a table, or you can sit on a stool at the _____.
22. The opposite of **yes**
24. A _____ is a person who buys something in a store, diner, or restaurant.
26. The opposite of **down**

17. The opposite of **always**
18. The first diners were _____ on the street.
21. Diners are open 24 hours a day. This means that diners are open around the _____ .
23. A _____ is a list of the food that you can choose to eat.
25. The opposite of **bottom**

## I. CLOZE Quiz

Ⓧ TEST

a     an     the

Read the passage below. Fill in each space with one of the articles listed above. You may use the words more than once.

In (1) ___THE___ late 1800s, long before (2) ___The___ first fast-food restaurants began, people ate at diners. At that time, diners were restaurants that served basic food quickly at (3) ___A___ reasonable price. Diners are (4) ___THE___ same today. However, early diners did not look like modern diners. First of all, they began as simple food carts. (5) ___AN___ old man named Walter Scott had (6) ___THE___ first "diner" in 1872. People on (7) ___THE___ street walked up to (8) ___THE___ cart to buy food. These carts served late-night workers who wanted (9) ___A___ cup of coffee and (10) ___A___ late-night meal. (11) ___THE___ meal was (12) ___A___ sandwich or (13) ___AN___ egg. In 1887, Samuel Messer Jones built (14) ___THE___ first diner big enough to allow (15) ___THE___ customers to come inside.

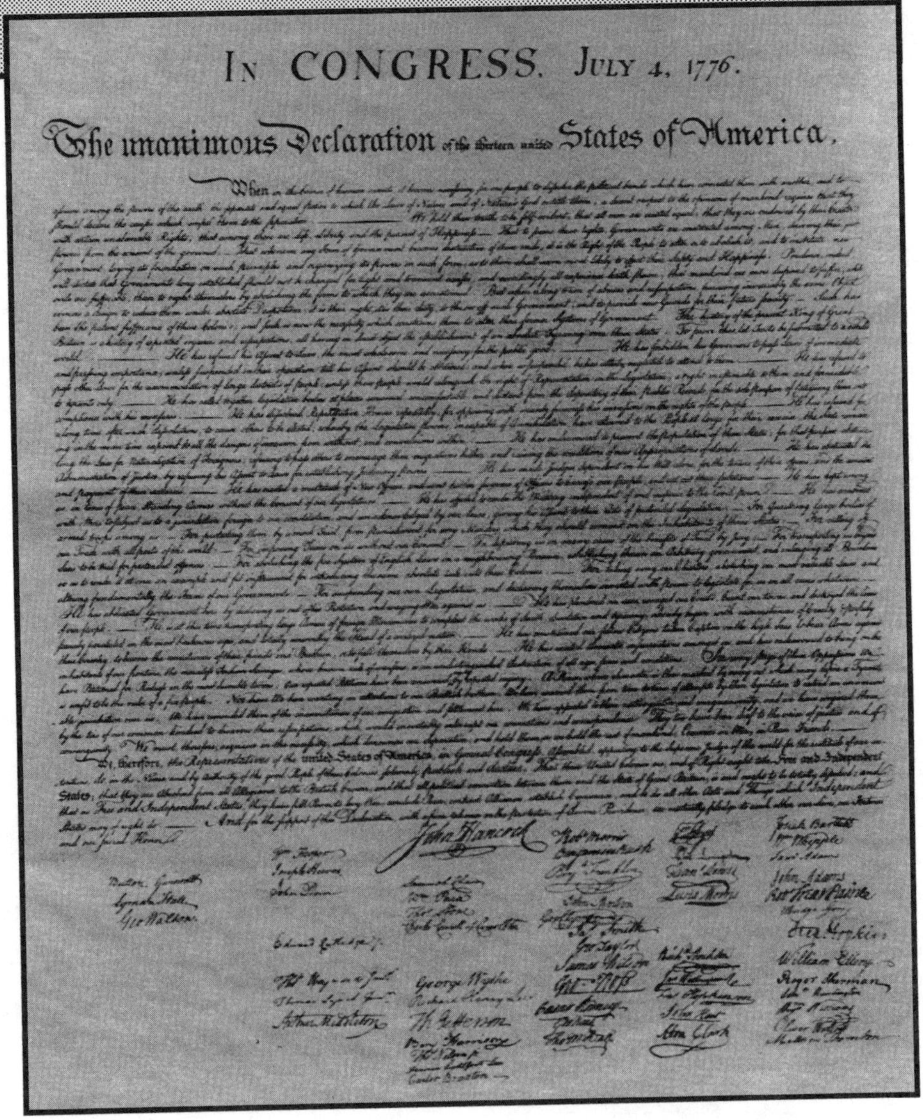
IN CONGRESS, JULY 4, 1776.

The unanimous Declaration of the thirteen united States of America,

# CHAPTER 4

# The Birth of the United States of America

## Prereading Preparation

1. Look at the photograph on the left. This is a photo of the Declaration of Independence. What is the Declaration of Independence?
2. When did the United States become independent?
3. Where is the United States of America?
4. Where did the people in the United States first come from?
5. Why did these people come to the United States?
6. Who was the first president of the United States? How did he become president?
7. Look carefully at the two maps illustrated on page 50. There are three differences between the original colonies and these states today. What are the three differences?

   1. _____

   2. _____

   3. _____

18th CENTURY COLONIES

20th CENTURY STATES

---

1    The United States is a big country. In fact, it is the fourth
2    largest country in the world. However, the United States
3    wasn't always so big. It began as a very small nation.

4    England had 13 colonies in North America in the 18th cen-
5    tury. The people who lived there were called colonists.
6    Naturally, the colonists were English. The British government
7    made the colonists pay taxes, but they had no one to represent    *đại diện*
8    them in the government. The colonists felt that this practice
9    was unfair.

10   The colonists wanted representation, so they decided to
12   create a congress. A congress is a group of representatives
13   who discuss problems. The Continental Congress had its first
14   meeting in secret on September 5, 1774. The congress did not
15   decide to fight for independence at this time, but war seemed
16   unavoidable. George III, the King of England, wanted the
17   colonists to obey him, but the colonists refused. The king did
18   not listen to the colonists' complaints. Finally, many people
19   felt that their only choice was to become independent. In June
20   1776, the Continental Congress organized the colonies into
21   states. Each state had its own government. A group of men
22   from each state met to write a public statement. Thomas
23   Jefferson was a member of this committee and was chiefly
24   responsible for writing this famous paper. It is called
25   the Declaration of Independence, and it is the basis of the

26 American government. On July 4, 1776, the colonists accepted
27 the Declaration. This date marked the beginning of the
28 American Revolution. The American Revolution was the war
29 between the American colonists and England. The colonists
30 fought for their independence from England.
31 　　When the war began, George Washington was already an
32 experienced military officer. People respected and admired
33 him. He was the commander-in-chief of the American army
34 during the American Revolution. During the war, the
35 Americans had few arms and clothes, and very little money.
36 The war was long and difficult, but finally the British signed a
37 peace treaty on September 3, 1783. A new nation was born.
38 　　The new country did not have a government. It only had the
39 Continental Congress, but the congress had no authority. For
40 example, it could not make laws or collect taxes to raise money.
41 Each state was very worried about keeping its own indepen-
42 dence. The states did not want a powerful central government.
43 The years 1783 to 1787 were very difficult ones for the new
44 nation. During these four years the states made many compro-
45 mises, and finally, on December 7, 1787, the states began to
46 accept the new Constitution and the new central government.
47 　　The Constitution created a formal Congress and a presi-
48 dent. The Congress unanimously elected George Washington
49 the first president of the United States. He was a good general
50 during the war, but most important, he was honest and fair,
51 and people trusted him. George Washington became president
52 on April 30, 1789, and the United States of America became
53 the first democracy in the world.

## A. Fact-Finding Exercise

Read the passage once. Then read the following statements. Check whether they are true (T) or false (F). If a statement is false, change the statement so that it is true. Then go back to the passage and find the line that supports your answer.

___ T  _X_ F  1. The United States is the largest country in the world.
*It is the fourth largest country in the world*

_X_ T  ___ F  2. The people who lived in the 13 colonies came from England.

_X_ T  ___ F  3. The King of England wanted the colonists in North America to pay taxes to England.

___ T  _X_ F  4. Thomas Jefferson wrote the Declaration of Independence alone.
*He wrote it with other people in a committee*

_✓_ T  ___ F  5. George Washington fought in the American Revolution.

___ T  _✓_ F  6. George Washington became the first president of the United States in 1776.
*George Washington became the first president in 1789.*

## B. Information Recall

Read the passage a second time. Then try to answer the following questions. Do not look back at the passage. Compare your answers with a classmate's answers.

1. Why did the colonists decide to become independent from England?
*They decided to become independent because the King did not listen to the colonists' complaints*

2. What was the purpose of the Continental Congress?
*The purpose of the continental congress was to give the colonists representation, and discuss problems*

3. Why was the Revolutionary War so difficult?
*It was so difficult because the Americans had few arms and clothes, and very little money, and because it was so long*

4.  Who was George Washington?

He was the commander-in-chief of the army during the American revolution, and he was the first president of the United States.

---

## C. Reading Analysis

Read each question carefully. Either circle the letter of the correct answer, or write your answer in the space provided.

1.  What is the main idea of this passage?
    a.  The United States had a revolution against England over 200 years ago.
    b.  The United States became a democratic country after a fight for independence.
    c.  The United States is the fourth largest country in the world.

2.  The United States is a big **country**. **In fact**, it is the fourth largest country in the world. However, the United States wasn't always so big. It began as a very small nation.
    a.  How many countries are bigger than the United States?
        1.  three
        2.  four
        3.  five
    b.  In this paragraph, which word is a synonym of **country**?

        nation

    c.  In this paragraph, what is the purpose of **in fact**?
        1.  It means the writer is telling the truth.
        2.  The second sentence gives more specific information than the first sentence about the actual size of the United States.
        3.  The second sentence gives different information from the first sentence.
    d.  Complete the following sentence correctly.

        My grandmother is a very old woman. In fact,
        1.  she has white hair and walks very slowly
        2.  she is 93 years old
        3.  she has ten grandchildren and five great-grandchildren

3.  England had 13 colonies in North America in the 18th century. The British government made the **English** colonists pay taxes, but they had no one to represent them in the government.
    a.  In this paragraph, which word is a synonym of **English**?

        BRITISH

b.  England had 13 **colonies** in North America. This means that England had 13
1.  communities of people ⟋
2.  businesses
3.  factories

4.  The Continental Congress had its first meeting in secret on September 5, 1774.
   a.  Was the first meeting of the Continental Congress probably legal or illegal?

   _____ *illegal.* _____

   b.  Why do you think so?

   *Because the first meeting was in Secret* _____

5.  The congress did not decide to fight for independence in 1774, but war seemed **unavoidable**.
   a.  This sentence means that
      ⟋1.  most people believed that war was going to happen
      2.  most people believed that war was not possible
   b.  Which of the following are unavoidable?
      ⟋1.  becoming older
      2.  becoming hungry
      ⟋3.  dying
      4.  getting married

6.  A group of men from each state met to write a public statement. Thomas Jefferson was a member of this **committee**.

   In this paragraph, **committee** means
   a.  several states that fight together
   ⟋b.  several people who get together to make decisions

7.  Thomas Jefferson was **chiefly** responsible for writing the Declaration of Independence. That is the reason why most people say he is the author of the Declaration.
   a.  These sentences mean that
      1.  many people helped Thomas Jefferson write the Declaration of Independence
      ⟋2.  Thomas Jefferson wrote the Declaration of Independence with very little help
   b.  In these sentences, **chiefly** means
      1.  only
      ⟋2.  mostly
      3.  completely

8. The Declaration of Independence is the **basis** of the American government. In this sentence, **basis** means
   a. reason; foundation ✓
   b. written part
   c. best part

9. Americans had **few arms** and clothes, and very little money.
   a. ✓1. Americans did not have many arms.
      2. Americans had a lot of arms.
   b. In this sentence, **arms** means
      1. the part of the body between the shoulder and the hand
   ✓2. weapons; for example, guns and cannons

10. The states made many **compromises** between 1783 and 1787.

   Read the following sentences.

   Walter wanted to go to an Italian restaurant. Effie wanted to go to a Chinese restaurant. They had an argument and stopped talking to each other.

   Joyce wants to stay out until 1 A.M. tonight. Her mother wants her to come home at 11 P.M. Joyce and her mother finally agree that Joyce can come home at midnight.
   a. Who made a compromise: Walter and Effie, or Joyce and her mother?

        *joyce and her mother*

   b. People make compromises when they
      1. make choices
   ✓2. make agreements
      3. make decisions

## D. Word Forms

### Part 1

In English, verbs change to nouns in several ways. Some verbs become nouns by adding the suffix *-ion* or *-ation*, for example, *elect* (v.), *election* (n.). Be careful of spelling changes, for example, *continue* (v.), *continuation* (n.).

Complete each sentence with the correct form of the words on the left. **Write all the verbs in the simple past tense. All the verbs are affirmative. All the nouns are singular.**

collect (v.)
collection (n.)

1. Last Saturday, we _____ all our newspapers and put them in a big box. The sanitation truck picked up the big, heavy _____ of newspapers and took it to a recycling center.

discuss (v.)
discussion (n.)

2. Maryanne had a serious _____ with her husband. They _____ their problem carefully before they made their decision.

create (v.)
creation (n.)

3. The Americans _____ a new form of government. Their special _____ is still working well.

decide (v.)
decision (n.)

4. Lee had a very difficult _____ to make. His company asked him to move to California from New York. He finally _____ to move to California.

organize (v.)
organization (n.)

5. At the beginning of the American Revolution, there was very little _____ in the American army. When George Washington _____ his Continental Army, he did not have much money.

declare (v.)
declaration (n.)

6. President Abraham Lincoln _____ Thanksgiving a national holiday. He made this happy _____ in 1864.

## Part 2

In English, the noun form and the verb form of some words are the same, for example, *change* (v.), *change* (n.).

Complete each sentence with the correct form of the word on the left. In addition, indicate whether you are using the verb (v.) or the noun (n.) form of each word. **Write all the verbs in the simple past tense. All the verbs are affirmative. All the nouns are singular.**

practice

1.  Joseph __practiced__ on the piano every day for two
    (v., n.)

    years. He became a good musician because of his daily

    _____.
    (v., n.)

compromise

2.  Judy wanted to go to a movie, but Mark wanted to stay
    home. They finally __compromised__. They watched
    (v., n.)

    a movie on television and decided to go out next
    week. Both Judy and Mark felt satisfied with their

    _____.
    (v., n.)

trust

3.  Mr. and Mrs. Akel had complete __trust__ in their
    (v., n.)

    children. They always __trusted__ their children to
    (v., n.)
    co trail uhien
    act responsibly.

respect

4.  Elizabeth did not like her boss, but she __respected__
    (v., n.)

    him very much. She had so much __respect__ for
    (v., n.)

    him because he worked so hard.

---

# E. Vocabulary in Context

arms (n.) *vũ khí*      few (adj.) *một vài*   refused (v.) *từ chối*
authority (n.) *quyền lực*  honest (adj.) *ngay thật*  unanimously (adv.) *đồng tâm nhất trí*
committee (n.) *bay chấp*  obeyed (v.) *tuân theo*  unavoidable (adj.) *không tránh được*
complaint (n.) *phàn nàn*            *bắt tuân phục*

Read each sentence below. Fill in each space with the correct word from the list above. Use each word only once.

1. Bernice is a member of the ___committee___ that organizes the yearly *everyone* office party.

2. No one likes to pay taxes, but we all have to pay them. Paying taxes is ___unavoidable___ .

3. Janet moved to Chicago from Florida two weeks ago. She has ___few___ friends in Chicago.

4. Fay asked Adrian to lend her $50, but he ___refused___ . Fay never pays back the money she borrows.

5. The food in Winnie's Restaurant is delicious, and everything is very clean. I only have one ___complaint___ . The restaurant is always very hot and smoky.

6. A police officer has the ___authority___ to arrest you if you break the law.

7. The teacher asked the students if they wanted to go home early. They answered ___unanimously___ , "Yes!" No one wanted to stay in school.

8. Tom ___obeyed___ the traffic light. He stopped on the red signal.

9. In England, police officers do not carry any ___arms___ , but in the United States, police officers always carry guns.

10. Sherwin is a very ___honest___ person. You can trust him to tell you the truth.

## F. Follow-up Activities

1.  Read through the passage again. Look for significant dates in U.S. history, and fill in the following time line. The first date is done as an example.

Time Line, 1750–1800

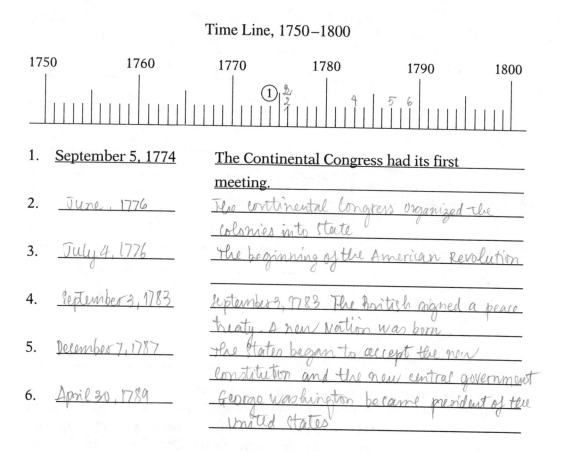

1.  <u>September 5, 1774</u>    <u>The Continental Congress had its first</u>

    <u>meeting.</u>

2.  <u>June, 1776</u>    <u>The continental Congress organized the</u>
    <u>colonies into state</u>

3.  <u>July 4, 1776</u>    <u>The beginning of the American Revolution</u>

4.  <u>September 3, 1783</u>    <u>September 3, 1783 The British signed a peace</u>
    <u>treaty. A new Nation was born.</u>

5.  <u>December 7, 1787</u>    <u>the States began to accept the new</u>
    <u>Constitution and the new central government</u>

6.  <u>April 30, 1789</u>    <u>George Washington became president of the</u>
    <u>United States</u>

2. Select five significant dates in the history of your country in the last three hundred years. Record the dates on the time line, and write the events on the lines below.

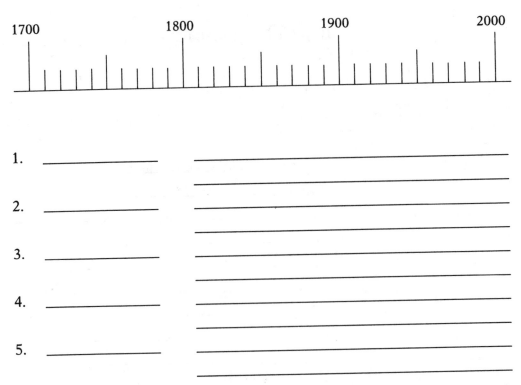

Time Line, 1700–2000

1. _____    _____

2. _____    _____

3. _____    _____

4. _____    _____

5. _____    _____

3. The new Americans accepted the Constitution, but they still worried. The Constitution did not clearly explain some basic rights, so members of the Continental Congress decided to make changes to the Constitution. They added specific rights to the Constitution in order to protect them forever. These changes in the Constitution are called amendments. The Bill of Rights is the name of the first ten amendments. The following rights are included in the Bill of Rights:
   1. Freedom of religion. Each person can practice any religion he or she wants.
   2. Freedom of speech. Each person has the right to say anything he or she wants if it is true.
   3. Freedom of the press. People have the right to print anything they want in newspapers and magazines if it is true.
   4. Freedom to have meetings. People have the right to meet together.
   5. Freedom to complain. Each person has the right to make a complaint to an official of the government.
   6. Freedom from unreasonable search. An officer must have a good reason to search a person's home.

7. Each person has the right to a fair trial by jury.
8. Each person can have the assistance of a lawyer.
9. Each person can have witnesses and can question witnesses who are against him.
10. Each person is guaranteed the protection of life, liberty, and property.

In groups, read the list of Rights. Discuss these rights, and put them in order of importance. In other words, the one you think is the most important is number 1. The one you think is the least important is number 10.

1. _____

2. _____

3. _____

4. _____

5. _____

6. _____

7. _____

8. _____

9. _____

10. _____

## G. Topics for Discussion and Writing

1. Get into groups with the students from your country. If no one else is from your country, you may work alone. Look back at the time line for your country. Choose one important event. Write about this event.

2. Today there are 50 states in the United States.
   a. In class, look at the map of the United States.
   b. Choose a state that you are interested in learning more about. Check your selection with your teacher to make sure that each student in the class chooses a different state.
   c. Together as a class, or in small groups, decide what information you want to learn about your states, for example, the population, the capital, the location, the date it became a state.
   d. Go to the library to get the information you need. Use the encyclopedia, or ask a librarian where to find more information.
   e. Prepare an oral presentation to tell the other students about your state.
   f. Prepare a written description of your state, which you will give to your teacher to read.

# The United States of America

3. Go to the encyclopedia or almanac in the library, and find out the exact size and population of your country. Prepare a chart with your classmates. List all the countries in order of size. Then list all the countries in order of population. Compare the two lists.

# H. Crossword Puzzle: The Birth of the United States

**Across Clues**

4. George Washington fought in many battles before the Revolutionary War. He was an _experienced_ general.
7. In a democracy, the people _elect_ the members of their government. The people vote for them.
10. The past tense of **have** _had_
11. There were one hundred people in the group. All one hundred people voted for John. They voted _unanimously_.
14. The past tense of **understand** _understood_
15. A _committee_ is a group of people who meet to solve problems.
16. Weapons, for example, guns and cannons _arms_

**Down Clues**

1. The past tense of **fall** _fell_
2. The past tense of **read** _read_
3. The past tense of **are** _were_
5. A _declaration_ is a public statement.
6. The past tense of **run** _ran_
8. The past tense of **show** _showed_
9. The past tense of **put** _put_
12. A _compromise_ is a way to settle a disagreement without an argument.
13. A _democracy_ is a form of government. The people choose the members of the government.
14. The colonists believed that war was going to happen. They believed that war was _unavoidable_.

17. The opposite of **off** *on*
18. ___*country*___ is another word for **nation**.
19. Mainly; mostly *chiefly*
20. The past tense of **see** *saw*
21. I believe in him. I ___*trust*___ him.
22. The past tense of **lie**, meaning **lie down** *lay*.
23. Foundation; reason *basis*
25. ___*British*___ is a synonym of **English.**

16. The Continental Congress needed power to make laws. It needed ___*authority*___.
18. Groups of people living in a new area but under the same government as before *colonies.*
22. The past tense of **lose** *lost*
24. You can have either coffee ___*or*___ tea. These are your two choices.

---

## I. CLOZE Quiz

at      in      on
for     of      to

Read the passage below. Fill in each space with one of the prepositions listed above. You may use the words more than once.

The colonists wanted representation, so they decided (1) ___to___ create a congress. A congress is a group (2) ___of___ representatives who discuss problems. The Continental Congress had its first meeting (3) ___in___ secret (4) ___on___ September 5, 1774. The congress did not decide (5) ___to___ fight (6) ___for___ independence (7) ___at___ this time, but war seemed unavoidable. George III, the King (8) ___of___ England, wanted the colonists (9) ___to___ obey him, but the colonists refused. The king did not listen (10) ___to___ the colonists' complaints. Finally, many people felt that their only choice was (11) ___to___ become independent. (12) ___in___ June 1776, the Continental Congress organized the colonies into states. Each state had its own government. A group (13) ___of___ men from each state met (14) ___to___ write a public statement. Thomas Jefferson was a member (15) ___of___ this committee and was chiefly responsible (16) ___for___ writing this famous paper. It is called the Declaration (17) ___of___ Independence, and it is the basis (18) ___of___ the American government. (19) ___on___ July 4, 1776, the colonists accepted the Declaration. (20) ___on___ September 3, 1783, the United States became independent.

---

## Unit II Discussion

The diner is uniquely American. Democracy began in the United States, too. Work with a classmate. What other examples can you give of something that is either uniquely American, or that began in the United States?

# UNIT III

## Family Life

# CHAPTER 5

## Twins: How Alike Are They?

### Prereading Preparation

1. Look at the photograph on the left. Describe the two men.
2. How are you and your brothers and sisters alike? Do you look alike? Do you like the same things? Do you have similar personalities?
3. How are you and your brothers and sisters different? Do you look different? Do you like different things? Do you have different personalities?
4. What are twins? Are they common? Do you know any twins? Are there twins in your family?
5. How are twins similar? Do they look alike? Are there different kinds of twins?
6. Do twins have the same personalities? Why, or why not?
7. Do you want to have twins? Why, or why not?

1　　Most twins who grew up together are very close. John and
2　Buell Fuller are 79-year-old identical twins. They have always
3　lived together, and still do. They wear identical clothes and
4　work together, too. They think it is funny that people can't tell
5　them apart. In fact, they like to confuse people. Sometimes
6　John tells people he is Buell, and sometimes Buell tells people
7　he is John.
8　　Identical twins like the Fullers are very unusual in the
9　United States. Out of every one thousand births, there are only
10　four pairs of identical twins. Naturally, most people are very
11　curious about them. Scientists want to know about twins, too.
12　Do twins feel the same pain? Do they think the same
13　thoughts? Do they share these thoughts?

14   Scientists understand how twins are born. Now, though,
15   they are trying to explain how being half of a biological pair
16   influences a twin's identity. They want to know why many
17   identical twins make similar choices even when they don't live
18   near each other. For example, Jim Springer and Jim Lewis are
19   identical twins. They were separated when they were only four
20   months old. The two Jims grew up in different families and
21   did not meet for 39 years. When they finally met, they discov-
22   ered some surprising similarities between them. Both men
23   were married twice. Their first wives were both named Linda,
24   and their second wives were both named Betty! Both twins
25   named their first sons James Allan, drove blue Chevrolets, and
26   had dogs named Toy. Are all these facts coincidences, or are
27   they biological?

28   Scientists want to know what influences personality. They
29   study pairs of identical twins who grew up in different sur-
30   roundings, like Jim Springer and Jim Lewis. These twins help
31   scientists understand the connection between environment
32   and biology. Researchers at the University of Minnesota stud-
33   ied 350 sets of identical twins who did not grow up together.
34   They discovered many similarities in their personalities.
35   Scientists believe that personality characteristics such as
36   friendliness, shyness, and fears are not a result of environ-
37   ment. These characteristics are inherited.

38   Some pairs of identical twins say that they have ESP*
39   experiences. For instance, some twins say that they can feel
40   when their twin is in pain or in trouble. Twins also seem to be
41   closer and more open to each other's thoughts and feelings
42   than other brothers and sisters. For example, Donald and
43   Louis Keith are close in this way. The Keiths are identical
44   twins. Donald says that by concentrating very hard, he can
45   make Louis telephone him.

46   Scientists continue to study identical twins because they
47   are uncertain about them and have many questions. However,
48   most twins are sure about one fact: being a twin is wonderful
49   because you are never alone and you always have a best
50   friend!

---

*ESP: Extrasensory Perception. ESP is the ability to feel something that
people cannot feel with the five senses.

## A. Fact-Finding Exercise

Read the passage once. Then read the following statements. Check whether they are true (T) or false (F). If a statement is false, change the statement so that it is true. Then go back to the passage and find the line that supports your answer.

___ T ___ F  1. Scientists want to know about identical twins.

_____

___ T ___ F  2. Jim Springer and Jim Lewis always lived together.

_____

___ T ___ F  3. Identical twins who grow up together help scientists understand them better.

_____

___ T ___ F  4. John and Buell Fuller were separated at birth and did not grow up together.

_____

___ T ___ F  5. Some identical twins have ESP experiences about each other.

_____

___ T ___ F  6. Friendliness, shyness, and fears are inherited.

_____

## B. Information Recall

Read the passage a second time. Then try to answer the following questions. Do not look back at the passage. Compare your answers with a classmate's answers.

1. How are Jim Springer and Jim Lewis similar?

_____

_____

2. a. Whom did the researchers at the University of Minnesota study?

_____

_____

  b. Why?

_____

_____

   c.   What did the researchers learn?

_____

_____

3.  How do the Fuller brothers confuse people? Why?

_____

_____

_____

4.  What kind of ESP experience did Donald and Louis Keith have?

_____

_____

_____

## C. Reading Analysis

Read each question carefully. Either circle the letter of the correct answer, or write your answer in the space provided.

1.  What is the main idea of this passage?
    a.   John and Buell Fuller, typical identical twins, grew up together.
    b.   Identical twins are very unusual in the United States.
    c.   Scientists believe that identical twins are very similar in both their looks and their personalities.

2.  Most twins who grew up together are very **close**. John and Buell Fuller are 79-year-old identical twins. They have always lived together, and **still do**. They wear identical clothes and work together, too. They think it is amusing that people **can't tell them apart**.
    a.   In this paragraph, **close** means that they
        1.  live near each other
        2.  live in the same house
        3.  are very good friends
    b.   What do John and Buell Fuller **still do**?
        1.  confuse people
        2.  live together
        3.  wear the same clothes
    c.   People **can't tell them apart**. This means that
        1.  they look exactly the same
        2.  people can't talk to them alone
        3.  they never work apart

3. Out of every one thousand births, there are only four pairs of identical twins.

    This means that
    a. if one thousand women have babies, four women will have identical twins
    b. only four pairs of identical twins are born in the United States every year

4. Most people **are very curious** about identical twins. Scientists want to know about twins, too. Do twins feel the same pain? Do they think the same thoughts? Do they share these thoughts?

    In these sentences, which word or phrase is a synonym of **are very curious**?
    a. feel
    b. want to know
    c. think

5. Scientists understand how twins are born. Now, though, they are trying to explain how **being half of a biological pair** influences a twin's identity.

    **Being half of a biological pair** means being
    a. a scientist
    b. a twin
    c. alone

6. Jim Springer and Jim Lewis are famous identical twins. They were separated when they were only four months old. **The two Jims** grew up in different families and did not meet for 39 years. **Both** men were married twice. Their first wives were both named Linda, and their second wives were both named Betty!
    a. Who are the **two Jims**?

    _____ Jim Springer and Jim Lewis _____
    b. How many is **both**?
       1. two
       2. four
       3. six

7. Both Jim Springer and Jim Lewis named their first sons James Allan. Both Jims drove blue Chevrolets. They both had dogs named Toy. Are all these facts simply **coincidences**?

Read the following sentences.
1. Dean telephoned Jenny and invited her to have lunch with him. They decided to meet at 1 o'clock on the corner of First Avenue and Main Street. At 1 o'clock, Jenny was on the corner, and Dean walked up to her. They said hello and went into the restaurant.
2. Dean and Jenny sat at a table in the restaurant. Jenny looked around the restaurant. Her sister, Christine, was at the next table! Jenny and Christine greeted each other, and they all had lunch together at the same table.
   a. Which situation was a coincidence: Dean and Jenny met on the corner at 1 o'clock, or Jenny met her sister in the restaurant?
      _____ *Jenny met her in the restaurant* _____
   b. A **coincidence** is something that happens
      1. by plan or arrangement
      2. by accident or chance ⁄
      3. on the street or in a restaurant

8. Scientists want to know what influences personality. **Pairs** of identical twins who grew up in different **surroundings**, like Jim Springer and Jim Lewis, help scientists understand the connection between environment and biology. Researchers at the University of Minnesota studied 350 sets of identical twins who did not grow up together.
   a. In this paragraph, which word is a synonym of **pairs**?
      _____ *Sets* _____
   b. In this paragraph, which word is a synonym of **surroundings**?
      _____ *neighborhood ; environment* _____
   c. What do these two words mean?
      1. the house you live in
      2. the place you live in
      3. the people you live with
      4. all of the above ⁄

9. Scientists believe that personality characteristics such as friendliness, shyness, and fears are not a result of environment. **They** are inherited.
   a. What are some examples of personality characteristics?

   _____ *friendly* _____

   b. How do you know?

   _____

   c. What does **they** refer to?
      1. scientists
      2. personality characteristics
      3. fears

10. Other pairs of identical twins say that they have **ESP** experiences.
    a. Look at line 38 of the passage. What is **ESP**?

    _____

    _____

    b. How do you know?

    _____

    c. This type of information is called a
       1. preface
       2. footnote
       3. direction

11. Donald and Louis Keith are very close. **The Keiths** are identical twins. Donald says that **by concentrating very hard, he can make Louis telephone him**.
    a. Who are **the Keiths**?

    _____ *Donald Keith and Louis Keith.* _____

    b. What does Donald mean?
       1. Donald tells Louis to call him, and Louis calls him.
       2. Donald thinks about Louis, and Louis calls him.

12. Scientists continue to study identical twins because they are **uncertain** about them and have many questions. However, most twins are sure about one fact: being a twin is wonderful because you are never alone and you always have a best friend!

    In this paragraph, which word means the opposite of **uncertain**?

    _____ *Sure* _____

## D. Word Forms

### Part 1

In English, adjectives change to nouns in several ways. Some adjectives become nouns by adding the suffix -*ness*, for example, *loud* (adj.), *loudness* (n.). Be careful of spelling changes, for example, *dry* (adj.), *dryness* (n.), but *happy* (adj.), *happiness* (n.).

Complete each sentence with the correct form of the words on the left. **The nouns are all singular.**

close (adj.)
closeness (n.)

1. Winnie and Loretta are good friends. They are very _____close_____ and tell each other everything. Their _____closeness_____ will continue for many years.

sure (adj.)
sureness (n.)

2. Jonathan is completely _____sure_____ that the movie begins at 9:30. His _____sureness_____ made us leave for the movie theater at 8:30.

open (adj.)
openness (n.)

3. Jimmy has a special _____openness_____ that many people like. He makes friends easily with his warm, _____open_____ personality.

friendly (adj.)
friendliness (n.)

4. All the people at Jodi's party are very _____friendly_____ to me. Their _____friendliness_____ makes me feel comfortable, and I'm having a good time.

shy (adj.)
shyness (n.)

5. Unfortunately, Raymond's _____shyness_____ stops him from making friends. He is too _____shy_____ to talk to people he doesn't know.

## Part 2

In English, the noun form and the verb form of some words are the same, for example, *cover* (v.), *cover* (n.).

Complete each sentence with the correct form of the word on the left. In addition, indicate whether you are using the verb (v.) or the noun (n.) form of each word. **Write all the verbs in the simple present tense. They may be affirmative or negative. The nouns may be singular or plural.**

influence

1. Our parents often have a strong _influence_ on our
   (v.,n.)
   lives. They usually _influence_ us in positive ways.
   (v.,n.)

fear

2. Tom has very few _fears_. However, when he
   (v.,n.)
   goes to bed, he always _fears_ that he will die in
   (v.,n.)
   his sleep.

experience

3. When a twin _experiences_ an ESP event, he usually calls
   (v.,n.)
   his twin to see if the twin had the same _experience_.
   (v.,n.)

work

4. Lisa _doesn't work_ at night. She only takes day jobs.
   (v.,n.)
   Her _work_ is very interesting. She writes
   (v.,n.)
   educational computer programs.

telephone

5. Please answer the _telephone_. It is ringing. I think it
   (v.,n.)
   is my brother. He always _telephones_ me at this time.
   (v.,n.)

## E. Vocabulary in Context

close (adj.)  identical (adj.)  pair (n.)
coincidence (n.)  influences (v.)  personality (n.)
concentrates (v.)  inherited (adj.)  similar (adj.)
environment (n.)

Read each sentence below. Fill in each space with the correct word from the list above. Use each word only once.

1. Our coats are very _similar_. They are blue and have a belt and four pockets. However, your coat is new and mine is old.

2. The weather _influences_ how we feel. For example, when it is cold and raining, we feel sad and tired. When it is cool and sunny, we feel happy and energetic.

3. Grace and her sister Emily do not get along well. They are not _close_ sisters.

4. When we describe socks, stockings, gloves, pants, and shoes, we usually say they are a _pair_.

5. Wendel always _concentrates_ very hard when he studies mathematics because it is the hardest subject for him.

6. These three boxes are _identical_. They are the same size, shape, color, and weight, and they are all made of wood.

7. Most plants need a lot of water. They also need a warm, sunny _environment_ in order to grow well.

8. James has a very pleasant _personality_. He is friendly, helpful, and intelligent. In addition, he is usually calm and happy.

9. My brown eyes are _inherited_ from my mother. She has brown eyes, too.

10. Last night Charles was writing a letter to his friend Harry when the telephone rang. Charles answered the phone. It was Harry! What a _coincidence_!

## F. Follow-up Activities

1. Work in pairs. Imagine you are going to interview a set of identical twins. These twins did not grow up together. In fact, they did not meet until they were 30 years old. Make up a list of questions to ask the twins. You want to find out how they are similar. Compare your list of questions with your classmates' lists.

2. Work in pairs. Imagine you are going to interview a set of identical twins. These twins *did* grow up together. Make up a list of questions to ask the twins. You want to find out how they are similar. Compare your list of questions with your classmates' lists.

3. If you can find a set of twins, interview them. Use the questions you have prepared. Report to the class.

## G. Topics for Discussion and Writing

1. Do you know any twins? Write about them. Tell who they are. Describe how they are alike and how they are different.
2. Explain why you think it is both good and bad to be a twin. Explain your good reasons and your bad reasons.
3. Imagine that you have a twin brother or sister. What do you like best about having a twin? What do you like least about having a twin?

## H. Crossword Puzzle: Twins

**Across Clues**

1. The opposite of **after**
5. A _____ is something that happens accidentally, without planning.
9. Saturday and Sunday are _____ days of the weekend.
11. Cats are very _____ animals. They want to know about everything.
12. Do you sit _____ all your classmates, or do you sit alone?
13. The opposite of **off**
14. The opposite of **up**
16. I will meet you _____ 6 o'clock
17. The color of your hair and your eyes are _____ from your parents.
19. _____ means **exactly the same.**

**Down Clues**

2. The opposite of **under**
3. I don't want to go to the movies alone. I want to go _____ you.
4. Your _____ is your character, your way of behaving.
5. Kathy and Laura are very good friends. They are very _____ .
6. When I think very hard about something, I _____ on it.
7. Our surroundings are our _____ .
8. Not together; apart
10. She does not like that idea. She is _____ it. She is not in favor of it.
15. The United States is _____ Canada and Mexico.

21. Not sure
23. A _____ is a person who studies something very carefully
24. The opposite of **above**
26. People cannot live _____ water.
27. The opposite of **in front of**

18. Our family, our education, and our home all have an _____ on us. They all affect us.
20. Almost alike; very close in appearance
22. I received a letter _____ my friend yesterday. Tomorrow I will write a letter to her.
25. The opposite of **in**
27. We come to class _____ bus.

## I. CLOZE Quiz

| he | they |
|----|------|
| him | them |
| his | their |

Read the passage below. Fill in each space with one of the pronouns listed above. You may use the words more than once.

Scientists understand how twins are born. Now, though, (1) _they_ are trying to explain how being half of a biological pair influences (2) _them_. (3) _They_ want to know why many identical twins make similar choices even when (4) _they_ don't live near each other. For example, Jim Springer and Jim Lewis are identical twins. Jim Springer was separated from Jim Lewis when (5) _they_ were only four months old. Jim Springer did not meet (6) _his_ brother Jim Lewis for 39 years. When Jim Springer finally met (7) _him_, (8) _he_ discovered some similarities between (9) _them_. Both men were married twice. (10) _Their_ first wives were both named Linda, and (11) _Their_ second wives were both named Betty! Both twins named (12) _Their_ first sons James Allan, drove blue Chevrolets, and had dogs named Toy. Are all these facts coincidences, or are (13) _They_ biological? How can we explain (14) _Them_?

# CHAPTER 6

## Adoption: The Search for Happiness

### Prereading Preparation

1. Look at the photograph on the left. Describe the man and the woman. Describe the baby. Does the baby look like the parents? Why, or why not?
2. What is **adoption**?
3. Why do some people adopt children?
4. Do most adopted children know their natural parents?
5. Can adopted children search for their natural parents? How?
6. Is adoption common in your country? Why, or why not?
7. What kinds of children do people adopt, for example, small babies, older children, boys, girls, children from different countries?
8. Do you know someone who is adopted? Does the adopted child have a happy life?
9. Do you know someone who adopted a child? Is the adoptive parent happy?

1　　When couples get married, they usually plan to have chil-
2　dren. Sometimes, however, a couple cannot have a child of
3　their own. In this case, they may decide to adopt a child. In
4　fact, adoption is very common today. There are about sixty
5　thousand adoptions each year in the United States alone.
6　Some people prefer to adopt infants; others adopt older chil-
7　dren. Some couples adopt children from their own countries;
8　others adopt children from foreign countries. Some people
9　adopt children of their same race, e.g., white, black, Asian.
10　Others adopt children of different races. In any case, they all

11  adopt children for the same reason: they care about children,
12  and want to give their adopted child a happy life. This includes
13  a comfortable home, a loving family, and a good education.
14      Most adopted children know that they are adopted.
15  Psychologists and child care experts generally think this is a
16  good idea. However, many adopted children, or adoptees, have
17  very little information about their biological mother and
18  father. As a matter of fact, it is often very difficult for adoptees
19  to find out about their birth parents because the birth records
20  of most adoptees are usually sealed. The information is confi-
21  dential, so no one can see it. Sealed documents protect both
22  adoptees and their natural parents.
23      Naturally, adopted children have different feelings about
24  their birth parents. Many adoptees want to search for them,
25  but others do not. Jake, who is 13, was adopted when he was
26  only two and a half months old. He says, "I don't think I'll ever
27  search for my birth mother. I might want to get some more
28  facts, but I don't feel I really want to go looking. Maybe she
29  would be awful, and I'd just be disappointed." Carla, who is
30  12, was adopted when she was four years old. Her adoptive
31  parents also adopted another little girl. Carla says,
32  "Sometimes my sister and I will talk. She says she doesn't
33  want to look for her birth mother when she gets older, but I
34  have mixed feelings. Sometimes I feel that I want to look for
35  her—and my mother says she'll help me when I'm older—but
36  sometimes I don't want to look for her at all because I'm
37  scared of finding out what her reactions would be. I worry
38  that she'll have a whole new life and I'll just be interfering with
39  that new life. She might not want anyone to know about her
40  past." Sue, who is 13, was adopted when she was a baby. Her
41  family helped her find her birth mother. Sue says, "I think
42  adopted kids should be allowed to search whenever they're
43  ready. They need to know where they came from. And they
44  need to know what their medical history is. As soon as I
45  searched and found the information I was looking for, I felt
46  more worthwhile in the world. Beforehand, a part of me had
47  always been missing."
48      The decision to search for birth parents is a difficult one to
49  make. Most adoptees, like Carla, have mixed feelings about
50  finding their biological parents. Even though adoptees do not
51  know about their past or their natural parents, they *do* know
52  that their adoptive parents want them, love them, and will
53  care for them.

## A. Fact-Finding Exercise

Read the passage once. Then read the following statements. Check whether they are true (T) or false (F). If a statement is false, change the statement so that it is true. Then go back to the passage and find the line that supports your answer.

___✓ T ___ F  1. Adoption is common in the United States.

_____

___ T ___ F  2. People only adopt babies of their same race.

*Some people adopt babies of different races*

___ T ___ F  3. Most adopted children don't know they are adopted.

*Most adopted children know they are adopted*

___ T ___ F  4. It is easy for adopted children to find their birth parents.

*It is difficult for adopted children to find their birth parents*

___✓ T ___ F  5. Most adoption birth records are confidential.

_____

___ T ___ F  6. Jake wants to find his birth mother.

*He does not want to look for her*

___✓ T ___ F  7. Sue found her birth mother.

_____

## B. Information Recall

Read the passage a second time. Then try to answer the following questions. Do not look back at the passage. Compare your answers with a classmate's answers.

1. Do all people adopt the same type of children? Explain your answer.

   *No, people adopt children ages, races and sexes*

2. Is it easy for adoptees to find their birth parents? Why, or why not?

   *No, birth records of most adopted children are usually sealed. (xai ding)*

3. Does Jake want to find his biological mother? Why, or why not?

   *No, He is afraid she would be awful, and he would be disappointed*

4. Does Carla want to find her biological mother? Why, or why not?

   *Sometimes she wants to look for her, but sometimes she doesn't*

5. Does Sue think it is a good idea for adoptees to find their birth parents? Why, or why not?

   *yes, They need to know where they came from, and they need to know what their medical history is*

## C. Reading Analysis

Read each question carefully. Either circle the letter of the correct answer, or write your answer in the space provided.

1. What is the main idea of this passage?
   a. Most adopted children know they are adopted, but not all of them want to find their natural parents.
   b. Some couples adopt children when they cannot have children of their own.
   c. People adopt children of different ages and races and from different countries.

2. When couples get married, they usually plan to have children. Sometimes, however, a couple cannot have a child of their own. **In this case**, they may decide to adopt a child. **In fact**, adoption is very common today. There are **about sixty thousand** adoptions **in the United States alone**.

   a.  **In this case** means
      1. ✓ when a couple cannot have children
      2.  when a couple plans to have children
      3.  when a couple gets married
   b.  What follows **in fact**?
      1.  an example of adoption
      2. ✓ more information about adoption
      3.  the reason for adoption
   c.  The last sentence means that
      1.  the United States is the only country in the world where people adopt children
      2. ✓ about sixty thousand adoptions take place in the United States, and many adoptions take place in other countries, too
      3.  people who adopt children in the United States are alone
   d.  What does **about sixty thousand** mean?
      1.  more than 60,000
      2.  less than 60,000
      3. ✓ around 60,000

3.  Some people prefer to adopt **infants**; others adopt older children.

What are **infants**?

_____ *babies* _____

4.  Some people adopt children of their same **race, e.g.,** white, black, Asian. Others adopt children of different races. **In any case**, they all adopt children for the same reason: they care about children, and want to give their adopted child a happy life. **This** includes a comfortable home, a loving family, and a good education.
   a.  What does **e.g.** mean?
      1. ✓ for example
      2.  the same race
      3.  also
   b.  What does **race** mean?

_____ *white, black, Asian* _____

   c.  What does **in any case** mean?
      1.  when people adopt children of the same race
      2. ✓ it does not matter what kind of child they adopt
      3.  if they adopt a child of a different race
   d.  What information follows the colon (:)?
      1.  the example
      2.  an opposite idea
      3. ✓ the reason

e.   What does **this** refer to?
1.   a good education
2. ⁄ a happy life
3.   a loving family

5. Most adopted children know that they are adopted. Psychologists and child care experts generally think **this** is a good idea.

What does **this** refer to?
a.   the fact that children know they are adopted
b.   the fact that people want to adopt children

6. Many adopted children, or **adoptees**, have very little information about their **biological mother and father**. **As a matter of fact**, it is often very difficult for adoptees to find out about their birth parents because the birth **records** of most adoptees are usually **sealed**. The information is **confidential**, so no one can see it. Sealed documents protect both adoptees and their natural parents.
a.   What does **adoptees** mean?
1.   adopted children
2.   adoptive parents
b.   How do you know?

_____

c.   In this paragraph, what are synonyms of the words **biological mother and father**?
1.   adoptees
2.   birth parents
3.   natural parents
4.   adoptive parents
5.   all of the above
6.   1 and 4
7.   2 and 3
8.   only 2
d.   What information follows **as a matter of fact**?
1.   more information about the same idea
2.   different information about the previous idea
3.   an example of the previous idea
e.   Which word in this paragraph is a synonym of **records**?

_____ documents _____

f.   What are **sealed** documents?
1.   They are documents that are in an envelope.
2.   They are documents that no one can read.

g. What does **confidential** mean?
1. important
2. serious
3. secret

7. **Naturally**, adopted children have different feelings about their birth parents. Many adoptees want to **search for** them, but others **do not**.
a. **Naturally** means
1. of course
2. however
3. biologically
b. **Search for** means
1. discover
2. look for
3. care for
c. What does **do not** mean?
1. Adoptees do not want to search for their birth parents.
2. Adoptees do not have different feelings about their birth parents.

8. Carla says, "My sister says she doesn't want to look for her birth mother, but I have **mixed feelings**. Sometimes I feel that I want to look for her—and my mother says she'll help me when I'm older—but sometimes I don't want to look for her because I'm scared of finding out what her reactions would be."
a. Why does Carla say that she has **mixed feelings**?
1. She does not want to look for her natural mother.
2. She wants to look for her natural mother.
3. She is not sure what she wants to do.
b. When you have **mixed feelings**, you
1. think two opposite ways about something
2. think differently from another person
c. What is between the two sets of dashes (—)?
1. information that explains the sentence
2. extra information that interrupts the sentence

9. She says, "Adopted kids need to know where they came from, and they need to know what their medical history is. As soon as I searched and found the information I was looking for, I felt more **worthwhile** in the world. **Beforehand**, a part of me had always been missing."
a. **Worthwhile** means
1. unsure
2. happy
3. important

b.   **Beforehand** means
   1.   before something happens
   2.   after something happens
   3.   because something happens

c.   Read the following sentence and complete it correctly.

Jack was on time when he arrived at the station to take the train. Beforehand,
   1.   he went to bed early last night
   2.   he called the station to find out the schedule

10.  **Even though** adoptees do not know about their past or their natural parents, they *do* know that their adoptive parents want them, love them, and will care for them.

a.   What does **even though** mean?
   1.   also
   2.   although
   3.   however

b.   Complete the following sentence.

Even though the train was late,
   1.   Karen arrived at work on time
   2.   Karen was late to work

c.   Why is **do** before the verb, and why is it italicized?
   1.   to show emphasis
   2.   to ask a question
   3.   to show an opinion

## D. Word Forms

**Part 1**

In English, verbs change to nouns in several ways. Some verbs become nouns by adding the suffix -*ion*, for example, *suggest* (v.), *suggestion* (n.).

Complete each sentence with the correct form of the words on the left. **Write all the verbs in the simple present tense. They may be affirmative or negative. The nouns may be singular or plural.**

decide (v.)
decision (n.)

1. Fred generally _decides_ where to go on vacation after he reads some travel books. As a matter of fact, Fred makes all his _decisions_ after he reads books or magazines.

inform (v.)
information (n.)

2. The Registrar's Office _doesn't inform_ students when they are accepted to a college. The Office of Admissions gives this _information_ .

react (v.)
reaction (n.)

3. John _doesn't react_ strongly when he is surprised or frightened. His _reactions_ are not usually easy to see.

protect (v.)
protection (n.)

4. An umbrella _doesn't protect_ you from the rain when the wind is blowing very hard. In this case, a raincoat gives better _protection_ .

adopt (v.)
adoption (n.)

5. When a couple _adopts_ a child, the family is usually happy. Before the _adoption_ takes place, the whole family usually discusses the decision together.

## Part 2

In English, the noun form and the verb form of some words are the same, for example, *visit* (v.), *visit* (n.).

Complete each sentence with the correct form of the word on the left. In addition, indicate whether you are using the verb (v.) or the noun (n.) form of each word. **Write all the verbs in the simple present tense. They may be affirmative or negative. The nouns may be singular or plural.**

plan
1. Terry has several _____*plan*_____ for his career. For example, he _____*plans*_____ to move to another city and to work
(v., n.)      (v., n.)

for the government.

care
2. All parents give love and _____*care*_____ to their children.
(v., n.)

In happy families, parents and children _____*care*_____
(v., n.)

about each other very much.

record
3. The Records Office at City Hall keeps all the _____*records*_____
(v., n.)

of births, marriages, and deaths, but it _____*doesn't record*_____
(v., n.)

sales of property. That information is in the Real Estate

Office.

search
4. When I lose my car keys, I usually _____*search*_____ for them
(v., n.)

in my pockets, but sometimes my _____*search*_____ is not
(v., n.)

successful. Then I look on the floor.

worry
5. Lee has many _____*worries*_____ about his family. However, he
(v., n.)

_____*doesn't worry*_____ about unimportant things.
(v., n.)

## E. Vocabulary in Context

as a matter of fact 4   includes (v.) 9   sealed (adj.) 10
beforehand (adv.) 3   mixed feelings 8   searches (v.) 5
confidential (adj.) 6   naturally (adv.) 1   worthwhile (adj.) 2
in any case 7

Read each sentence below. Fill in each space with the correct word from the list above. Use each word only once.

1. Helen is a happy, friendly, helpful person. _Naturally_, she is very popular.

2. Don't spend your time watching television all day. Do something _Worthwhile_. For example, read an interesting book, visit a museum, or see a good movie.

3. You will surely pass your English test if you study carefully _beforehand_.

4. I'm sure that Kevin is back from his vacation. _As a matter of fact_, he telephoned me this morning.

5. If Tom loses something, he _searches_ everywhere until he finds it.

6. Your medical records are usually _confidental_. Your doctor will not discuss them with anyone except you.

7. Sometimes Ann studies alone. At other times, she studies with other students. Occasionally, she does her homework with one other student. _in any case_, Ann works very hard to get good grades.

8. Carlo has _mixed_ about studying in a foreign university. He will get a good education, but he will miss his family and friends.

9. The price of the house _includes_ the refrigerator, stove, washing machine, clothes dryer, and air conditioners.

10. Some government documents are _sealed_ for 50 years. After that time, people can ask to see them.

## F. Follow-up Activities

1. Work with another student.

   **Student A:** You are an adoptee. You were adopted when you were six months old. You are meeting your biological mother for the first time.

   **Student B:** You are student A's natural mother/father. You are meeting your biological child for the first time since he/she was six months old.

   Write a dialogue. Introduce yourselves to each other. Then have a conversation. What will you say to each other? What questions will you ask each other? Share your dialogue with the class.

2. Work with a partner. Pretend that you want to adopt a child. What kind of child do you want? Describe the child's age, race, sex, etc. Why do you want to adopt this particular kind of child? What kind of life do you want for your adopted child?

## G. Topics for Discussion and Writing

1. Do you think it is a good idea for adoptees to search for their birth parents? Explain your answer.
2. Do you think it is a good idea for people to adopt children who are a different race? Explain your answer.
3. In your country, can anyone adopt a child? For example, can a single man adopt a child? Do you think it is a good idea for anyone—male, female, married or single—to adopt a child? Explain your answer.
4. Imagine that you are married, and you cannot have children of your own. Will you adopt children? If you will, why is it important for you to have children? If you won't, explain your reasons.
5. People sometimes give up their children for adoption. Imagine that you are going to give up your child. Write a letter to your best friend and explain your reasons.

## H. Crossword Puzzle: Adoption

### Across Clues

1. I ate my food, and the dog ate _____ food.
5. _____ means make a child part of your family.
7. Response
8. I didn't eat anything all day. _____ , I'm very hungry.
12. The time before something happens.
15. White, black, Asian: each one is a _____ .
16. At the present time
18. Adopted children
19. Closed; no one can see
21. Two people, usually a man and a woman
22. I have my books, and they have _____ books.
23. I didn't sleep well last night. I am _____ tired.

### Down Clues

1. Babies
2. Make up your mind about something.
3. She likes her teacher. He likes _____ teacher, too.
4. Secret
6. We all have _____ own homes.
9. The opposite of **no**
10. Valuable
11. Look for
13. Biological mother and father
14. Records; important papers
17. She lost _____ bag.
20. You passed _____ test!
21. Parents _____ about their children.

## I. CLOZE Quiz

| I | she | they |
|---|-----|------|
| me | her | them |
| my | her | their |

Read the passage below. Fill in each space with one of the pronouns listed above. You may use the words more than once.

Naturally, adopted children have different feelings about (1) __their__ birth parents. Many adoptees want to search for (2) __them__ , but others do not. (3) __they__ have different feelings. Jake says, "(4) __I__ don't think (5) __I__ will ever search for (6) __my__ birth mother. (7) __I__ might want to get some more facts, but (8) __I__ don't feel (9)__I__ really want to go looking." Carla was adopted when (10) __she__ was four years old. (11) __Her__ adoptive parents also adopted another little girl. Carla says, "Sometimes (12) __my__ sister and (13) __I__ will talk. (14) __she__ says (15) __she__ doesn't want to look for (16) __her__ birth mother when (17) __she__ gets older, but (18) __I__ have mixed feelings. Sometimes (19)__I__ feel that (20) __I__ want to look for (21) __her__ , and (22) __my__ mother says (23) __she__ will help (24) __me__ when (25) __I__ am older."

## Unit III Discussion

Some twins do not grow up together because they live with different families. Sometimes these twins are adopted separately. Is this a good idea? Explain your answer.

# UNIT IV
## Healthy Living

# CHAPTER 7

## Secondhand Smoke

---

### Prereading Preparation

1. Look at the photograph on the left. Describe what is happening. Is the man breathing in cigarette smoke, too? Is this healthy or unhealthy for him?
2. Do you smoke cigarettes? Do you know people who smoke?
3. Why do people smoke?
4. Is smoking good for you? Why, or why not?
5. What are some serious effects of smoking?
6. Is cigarette smoke only harmful to smokers? Why, or why not?
7. Is cigarette smoke harmful to nonsmokers? Why, or why not?
8. If you don't smoke, how do you feel about smoking? Does it bother you? Why, or why not?
9. Do you know of any laws about smoking? Where can people smoke? Where can't people smoke? Can you smoke here? Why, or why not?

1  Most people know that cigarette smoking is harmful to
2  their health. Scientific research shows that it causes many
3  kinds of diseases. In fact, many people who smoke get lung
4  cancer. However, Edward Gilson has lung cancer, and he has
5  never smoked cigarettes. He lives with his wife, Evelyn, who
6  has smoked about a pack of cigarettes a day throughout their
7  marriage. The Gilsons have been married for 35 years.
8      No one knows for sure why Mr. Gilson has lung cancer.
9  Nevertheless, doctors believe that secondhand smoke may

10  cause lung cancer in people who do not smoke. Nonsmokers
11  often breathe in the smoke from other people's cigarettes. This is
12  secondhand smoke. Edward Gilson has been breathing this type
13  of smoke for 35 years. Now he is dying of lung cancer. However,
14  he is not alone. The U.S. Environmental Protection Agency*
15  reports that about fifty-three thousand people die in the United
16  States each year as a result of exposure to secondhand smoke.

17      The smoke that comes from a lit cigarette contains many
18  different poisonous chemicals. In the past, scientists did not
19  think that these chemicals could harm a nonsmoker's health.
20  Recently, though, scientists changed their opinion after they
21  studied a large group of nonsmokers. They discovered that
22  even nonsmokers had unhealthy amounts of these toxic chem-
23  icals in their bodies. As a matter of fact, almost all of us
24  breathe tobacco smoke at times, whether we realize it or not.
25  For example, we cannot avoid secondhand smoke in restau-
26  rants, hotels, and other public places. Even though many pub-
27  lic places have nonsmoking areas, smoke flows in from the
28  areas where smoking is permitted.

29      It is even harder for children to avoid secondhand smoke.
30  In the United States, nine million children under the age of five
31  live in homes with at least one smoker. Research shows that
32  these children are sick more often than children who live in
33  homes where no one smokes. The damaging effects of second-
34  hand smoke on children also continue as they grow up. The
35  children of smokers are more than twice as likely to develop
36  lung cancer when they are adults as children of nonsmokers.
37  The risk is even higher for children who live in homes where
38  both parents smoke.

39      People are becoming very aware of the danger of second-
40  hand smoke. As a result, they have passed laws that prohibit
41  people from smoking in many public places. Currently, 45
42  states in the United States have laws that restrict, or limit,
43  smoking. The most well-known law forbids people to smoke on
44  short domestic airline flights, i.e., flights within the country.

45      After smoking for most of her life, Evelyn Gilson has finally
46  quit. She feels that if more people know about the dangers of
47  secondhand smoke, they will stop, too. Her decision comes too
48  late to help her husband. However, there is still time to protect
49  the health of others, especially children, who live with smokers.

---

*Environmental Protection Agency (EPA): A government department that is
responsible for protecting the U.S. environment, particularly the air and
water.

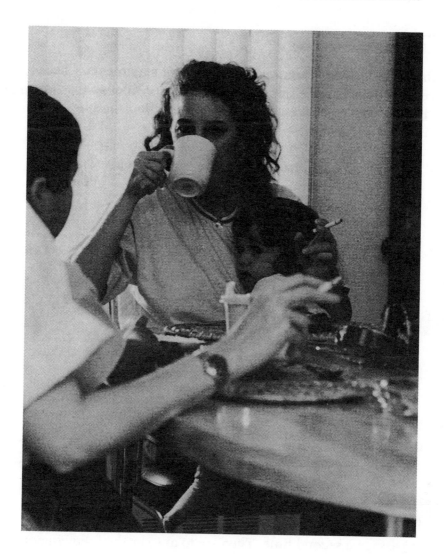

## A. Fact-Finding Exercise

Read the passage once. Then read the following statements. Check whether they are true (T) or false (F). If a statement is false, change the statement so that it is true. Then go back to the passage and find the line that supports your answer.

____ T ____ F  1. Cigarette smoking causes many diseases.

____ T ____ F  2. Evelyn Gilson has lung cancer.

*Her husband has lung cancer*

____ T ____ F  3. Secondhand smoke is the smoke from other people's cigarettes.

*Many people die from second hand Smoke*

____ T ____ F  4. People do not die from secondhand smoke.

____ T ____ F  5. Children of smokers are sick more often than children of nonsmokers are.

____ T ____ F  6. In the United States, you cannot smoke on any domestic airline flights.

*You cannot smoke on short domestic airlines flights*

## B. Information Recall

Read the passage a second time. Then try to answer the following questions. Do not look back at the passage. Compare your answers with a classmate's answers.

1. What may be a reason why Edward Gilson has lung cancer?

_____

_____

2. a.  What is secondhand smoke?

_____

_____

 b.  Why might it harm nonsmokers?

_____

_____

3. a. Why is it harder for children to avoid secondhand smoke than it is for adults?

   _____

   _____

   b. What are some effects of secondhand smoke on children?

   _____

   _____

4. What are some laws that prohibit smoking in certain places?

   _____

   _____

## C. Reading Analysis

Read each question carefully. Either circle the letter of the correct answer, or write your answer in the space provided.

1. What is the main idea of this passage?
   a. Edward Gilson has lung cancer, but he has never smoked.
   b. Secondhand smoke is very harmful to nonsmokers.
   c. Nonsmokers often breathe in secondhand smoke.

2. Scientific research shows that cigarette smoking causes many kinds of diseases. **In fact**, many people who smoke get lung cancer.

   What kind of information follows **in fact**?
   a. more specific information about the idea in the sentence before
   b. new, different information from the idea in the sentence before

3. No one knows **for sure** why Mr. Gilson has lung cancer. **Nevertheless**, doctors believe that secondhand smoke may cause lung cancer in people who do not smoke.
   a. **For sure** means
      1. definitely
      2. for example
      3. right now
   b. **Nevertheless** means
      1. in addition
      2. however
      3. in fact

4. Nonsmokers often breathe in the smoke from other people's cigarettes. This is secondhand smoke. Edward Gilson has been breathing **this type of smoke** for 35 years. Now he is dying of lung cancer. **However,** he is not alone. The U.S. **Environmental Protection Agency** reports that about fifty-three thousand people die in the United States each year as a result of exposure to secondhand smoke.

   a. What does **this type of smoke** refer to?

   *Secondhand smoke*

   b. **However** means
      1. but ✓
      2. and
      3. so

   c. **He is not alone.**

      This sentence means that
      1. his wife is also dying of lung cancer
      2. his wife and family are with him
      3. other nonsmokers are dying of lung cancer ✓

   d. Look at line 14 of the passage. What is the **Environmental Protection Agency?**

   *It is a government department that is responsible for protecting the U.S. environment, particularly the air and water*

   e. How do you know?

   f. This type of information is called a(n)
      1. index
      2. footnote ✓
      3. preface

5. In the past, scientists did not think that the chemicals in cigarette smoke could harm a nonsmoker's health. Recently, though, **scientists changed their opinion** after they studied a large group of nonsmokers.

   What is the scientists' opinion now?
   a. Cigarette smoke can harm a nonsmoker's health. ✓
   b. Cigarette smoke cannot harm a nonsmoker's health.

6. The smoke that comes from a lit cigarette contains many different **poisonous** chemicals. Scientists discovered that even nonsmokers had unhealthy amounts of these toxic chemicals in their bodies. **As a matter of fact,** almost all of us breathe tobacco smoke at times.

a.   In this paragraph, which word is a synonym of **poisonous**?

_____ toxic

b.   What does **as a matter of fact** mean?
1.   however
2.   in fact ⁄
3.   in addition

7.  **Even though** many public places have nonsmoking areas, smoke flows in from the areas where smoking is permitted.
   a.   What does **even though** mean?
   1.   because
   2.   as a result
   3.   although ⁄
   b.   Read the following sentences. Write the words **even though** in the correct space.
   1. ⁄ Bob went to school ___even Though___ he was sick.
   2.   Bob went to the doctor's office ___because___ he was sick.

8.  It is even harder for children to avoid secondhand smoke.

   This sentence means
   a. ⁄ it is easier for adults to stay away from secondhand smoke
   b.   it is easier for children to stay away from secondhand smoke

9.  In the United States, nine million children under the age of five live in homes with **at least** one smoker. Research shows that these children are sick more often than children who live in homes where no one smokes.

   **At least** means
   a. ⁄ a minimum of
   b.   less than
   c.   more than

10. The children are **more than twice as likely** to develop lung cancer when they are adults as children of nonsmokers.

   This sentence means that, compared to the children of nonsmokers,
   a. ⁄ children of smokers have double the chance of developing lung cancer
   b.   children of smokers will develop lung cancer more quickly

11. People are becoming very aware of the danger of secondhand smoke. **As a result**, they have passed laws which **prohibit** people from smoking in many public places. **Currently**, 45 states in the United States have laws that **restrict**, or limit, smoking. The most well-known law forbids people to smoke on short **domestic** airline flights, **i.e.**, flights within the country.

    a. **As a result** means
        1. in addition
        2. however
        3. consequently

    b. In this paragraph, which word is a synonym of **prohibit**?

        *forbid.*

    c. What does **currently** mean?
        1. recently
        2. right now
        3. in the future

    d. In this paragraph, which word is a synonym of **restrict**?

        *limit*

    e. How do you know?

    f. What information follows **i.e.**?
        1. an explanation
        2. a reason
        3. an example

    g. What is a **domestic** flight?

        *a flight within a country*

## D. Word Forms

### Part 1

In English, the noun form and the verb form of some words are the same, for example, **cause** (v.), **cause** (n.).

Complete each sentence with the correct form of the word on the left. In addition, indicate whether you are using the verb (v.) or the noun (n.) form of each word. **Write all the verbs in the simple present tense. They may be affirmative or negative. The nouns may be singular or plural.**

report
1. Mark writes several short ___reports___ on public
   (v., n.)

   health every month. He usually ___reports___ on
   (v., n.)

   nutrition and exercise.

damage
2. Direct exposure to the sun ___damages___ the eyes.
   (v., n.)

   Consequently, never look directly into the sun in

   order to avoid any chance of eye _____ .
   (v., n.)

limit
3. If smoking parents ___do not limit___ their children's
   (v., n.)

   exposure to cigarette smoke, the children will have

   a much higher risk of becoming sick. Parents need

   to put a definite _____ on the amount of
   (v., n.)

   smoking they do at home.

study
4. The EPA publishes its ___studies___ when they
   (v., n.)

   are complete. The EPA ___studies___ the quality
   (v., n.)

   of air and water in the United States.

result
5. Smoking cigarettes ___does not result___ in lung cancer
   (v., n.)

   for every smoker. For example, Evelyn Gilson

   does not have lung cancer. However, the usual

   ___results___ of smoking are frequent colds,
   (v., n.)

   bronchitis, and other diseases of the lungs.

## Part 2

In English, some adjectives become nouns by adding the suffix -ness, for example, quick (adj.), quickness (n.).

Complete each sentence with the correct form of the words on the left. **The nouns may be singular or plural.**

sick (adj.)

sickness (n.)

1. Phil was quite ___sick___ last month. Because his _____ was very severe, he stayed in bed for three weeks.

aware (adj.)

awareness (n.)

2. Lisa wanted me to be ___aware___ of the heavy traffic on the highway. My _____ of driving conditions saved me a lot of time.

near (adj.)

nearness (n.)

3. The curious dog came very ___near___ the small child. The little girl was uncomfortable with the _____ of such a big animal, and she began to cry.

late (adj.)

lateness (n.)

4. The teacher has strict rules about being ___late___. In fact, if a student has several _____, she will not allow him in class any more.

weak (adj.)

weakness (n.)

5. Alice went to the doctor because she had _____ in her legs. The doctor told her that she felt ___weak___ because she didn't exercise enough.

## E. Vocabulary in Context

| | | |
|---|---|---|
| as a matter of fact | harmful (adj.) | realizes (v.) |
| avoids (v.) | nevertheless (adv.) | recently (adv.) |
| disease (n.) | prohibits (v.) | toxic (adj.) |
| exposure (n.) | | |

Read each sentence below. Fill in each space with the correct word from the list above. Use each word only once.

1. Many people limit their ___exposure___ to the sun because their skin burns very easily.

2. I think that Wayne ___realizes___ he cannot pass the exam. He didn't study for it.

3. Many chemicals that kill insects are also ___toxic___ to humans.

4. Chris is a very popular artist. _____, several of his paintings are on exhibit at the City Art Museum.

5. I don't think I can win a tennis game against Stella. ___nevertheless___, I will try to play as well as I can.

6. The new state law ___prohibits___ the sale of alcohol to people under 21 years of age.

7. Barbara was always very quiet and shy, but ___recently___ she has started to become more sociable.

8. Bronchitis is one type of ___disease___ that smokers may develop.

9. The _____ effects of smoking may take many years to develop.

10. Emily usually ___avoids___ the State Parkway because there are always too many cars.

## F. Follow-up Activities

1. Work with another student in this role play.

   **Student 1:** You are a nonsmoker. You are sitting in a restaurant. The person sitting at the table next to you is smoking. Politely ask that person to put out the cigarette.

   **Student 2:** You are a smoker. You are sitting in a restaurant smoking a cigarette. The person at the next table politely asks you to put out your cigarette. Respond to the person's request.

2. Work in small groups. Pretend that you are the lawmakers in your city, state, or country. Make up laws about smoking. Decide where people can smoke and where they cannot smoke. Present your laws to the class. Give reasons for your decisions.

3. Work in small groups. You represent smokers. You do not want new laws that prohibit smoking. Prepare reasons why you think prohibiting smoking is a bad idea.

4. Advertisements are designed to make people want to buy and use a particular product. Look through magazines and newspapers for a cigarette advertisement. Bring it to class. In groups, discuss the advertisement. Why might it make someone want to buy and smoke cigarettes? What do you think of these reasons?

5. Work in pairs or small groups. You are an advertiser for a tobacco company. Design an advertisement for your cigarette.

6. Work in pairs or small groups. You are on the Committee for Public Health. Design an advertisement to show the dangers of smoking.

## G. Topics for Discussion and Writing

1. Many people believe that people have a right to smoke wherever they want. Do you agree or disagree with this opinion? Explain your answer.

2. Many people believe that cigarettes should be illegal, just like marijuana or certain drugs. Do you agree or disagree with this opinion? Why?

3. Are there laws in your country about smoking? List them. Compare the laws in your country with the laws in your classmates' countries.

4. Do you think it is right for a government to tell people where they can or cannot smoke? Why, or why not?

## H. Crossword Puzzle: Secondhand Smoke

### Across Clues
1. Try to stay away from
4. Two times
5. 20 cigarettes in one box is a _____ of cigarettes.
6. The opposite of **bottom**
9. _____ smoke is the type of smoke you breathe in from someone else's cigarette.
12. Forbid; not allow
14. That is
15. Toxic
17. The opposite of **pull**
18. Cigarettes are made from this plant.
21. Schools, libraries, and restaurants are _____ places.
22. At the present time
23. The opposite of **come**

### Down Clues
1. I _____ . You are.
2. This word refers to activities within a country.
3. Chance
7. A very serious disease
8. Dangerous
10. _____ though I studied, I did not pass the exam.
11. Someone who does not smoke is a _____ .
13. A disease of the lungs
16. The opposite of **sick**
19. Stop
20. When we breathe, air enters our _____ .

## I. CLOZE Quiz

for    in    of    to

Read the passage below. Fill in each space with one of the prepositions listed above. You may use the words more than once.

Most people know that cigarette smoking is harmful (1) __to__ their health. Scientific research shows that it causes many kinds (2) __of__ diseases. (3) __In__ fact, many people who smoke get lung cancer. However, Edward Gilson has lung cancer, and he has never smoked cigarettes. He lives with his wife, Evelyn, who has smoked about a pack (4) __of__ cigarettes a day throughout their marriage. The Gilsons have been married (5) __for__ 35 years.

No one knows (6) __for__ sure why Mr. Gilson has lung cancer. Nevertheless, doctors believe that secondhand smoke may cause lung cancer (7) __in__ people who do not smoke. Nonsmokers often breathe (8) __in__ the smoke from other people's cigarettes. This is second-hand smoke. Edward Gilson has been breathing this type (9) __of__ smoke for 35 years. Now he is dying (10) __of__ lung cancer. However, he is not alone. The U.S. Environmental Protection Agency reports that about fifty-three thousand people die (11) __in__ the United States each year as a result (12) __of__ exposure (13) __to__ secondhand smoke.

# CHAPTER 8

# A Healthy Diet for Everyone

---

## Prereading Preparation

1. Look at the photograph on the left. Describe the two meals. Which meal do you think is healthier? Why?
2. Do you eat healthy food all the time?
3. What kind of food is good you for? Make a list.

   _____      _____

   _____      _____

   _____      _____

4. What kind of food is bad for you? Make a list.

   _____      _____

   _____      _____

   _____      _____

5. What does **a healthy diet** mean?
6. Why is it important to have a healthy diet?
7. Do most people in your country have a healthy diet? Why, or why not?

---

1    Sometimes, people are confused about what type of food is
2  healthy, and what kind of food can be bad for our health. In
3  1956, the USDA* described four basic food groups: meat
4  (meat, fish, chicken, etc.), dairy (cheese, butter, etc.), grains
5  (bread, cereals, rice, etc.), and fruit and vegetables. The USDA
6  suggested how much of each food group was healthy to eat
7  daily. Now, however, these suggestions are changing. The four
8  food groups are still the same, but the amounts from each
9  food group are different.

10     As a result of years of research, we know that too much
11 animal fat is bad for our health. For example, Americans eat a
12 lot of meat and only a small amount of grains, fruit, and veg-
13 etables. Because of their diet, they have high rates of cancer
14 and heart disease. In Japan, in contrast, people eat large
15 amounts of grains and very little meat. The Japanese also
16 have very low rates of cancer and heart disease. In fact,
17 the Japanese live longer than anyone else in the world.
18 Unfortunately, when Japanese people move to the United
19 States, their rates of heart disease and cancer increase as their
20 diet changes. Moreover, as hamburgers, ice cream, and other
21 high-fat foods become popular in Japan, the rates of heart dis-
22 ease and cancer are increasing there as well. People are also
23 eating more meat and dairy products in other countries such
24 as Cuba, Mauritius, and Hungary. Not surprisingly, the disease
25 rates in these countries are increasing along with the change
26 in diet. Consequently, doctors everywhere advise people to eat
27 more grains, fruit, and vegetables, and to eat less meat and
28 fewer dairy products.

29     A healthy diet is important for children as well as adults.
30 When adults have poor eating habits, their children usually
31 do, too. After all, children eat the same way as their parents.
32 When parents eat healthy food, the children will think it tastes
33 good. Then they will develop good eating habits. Doctors
34 advise parents to give their children healthier snacks such as
35 fruit, vegetables, and juice.

36     Everyone wants to live a long, healthy life. We know that
37 the food we eat affects us in different ways. For instance, doc-
38 tors believe that fruit and vegetables can actually prevent
39 many different diseases. On the other hand, animal fat can
40 cause disease. We can improve our diet now, and enjoy many
41 years of healthy living.

*Moreover, besides
in addition*

*disease bệnh tật*

---

*USDA: U.S. Department of Agriculture. Its responsibility is to control the
quality of food in the United States.

## A. Fact-Finding Exercise

Read the passage once. Then read the following statements. Check whether they are true (T) or false (F). If a statement is false, change the statement so that it is true. Then go back to the passage and find the line that supports your answer.

___ *l* T ___F   1. There are four basic food groups.

___ T ___F   2. The food groups are changing.
*The amount of each food group to eat is changing*

___ *,* T ___F   3. Most Americans eat a lot of meat.

___ T ___F   4. Most Japanese eat very few grains.   *little meat*
*Most Japanese eat a lot of grains. Or most Japanese eat very*

___ T ___F   5. There are high rates of cancer and heart disease
in Japan.   *heart*
*There are very slow rates of cancer and disease in Japan*

___ ✓ T ___F   6. Doctors think it is a good idea for people to eat
less meat.

___ T ___F   7. It is not important for children to have a healthy diet.
*It is very*

___ T ___F   8. Children usually eat differently than their parents.
*The same way*

___ T ___F   9. Doctors believe that fruit and vegetables cause
different diseases.
*prevent*

## B. Information Recall

Read the passage a second time. Then try to answer the following questions. Do not look back at the passage. Compare your answers with a classmate's answers.

1. a.   Do Americans have high rates of cancer and heart disease?
*yes*

   b.   Why, or why not?
*because they eat a lot of meat and only a small*
*amount of grains, fruit and vegetables*

2. a. Do Japanese have high rates of cancer and heart disease?

   *no*

   b. Why, or why not?

   *because they eat a lot of grains and very little meat*

3. a. What sometimes happens when Japanese people move to the United States?

   *their rates of cancer and heart disease increase*

   b. Why does this happen?

   *because their diet change*

4. a. What is happening to the disease rates in Cuba, Mauritius, and Hungary?

   *the disease rates in these countries are increasing.*

   b. Why is this happening?

   *Because the diets of people in these country are changing*

5. a. What effects can eating fruit and vegetables have on some diseases?

   *Eating fruit and vegetables can prevent some disease*

   b. What effects can eating meat have on some diseases?

   *Eating meat can cause some disease.*

---

## C. Reading Analysis

Read each question carefully. Either circle the letter of the correct answer, or write your answer in the space provided.

1. What is the main idea of this passage?
   a. The kind of diet we have can cause or prevent diseases.
   b. Doctors advise people to eat more fruit, vegetables, and grains.
   c. Eating meat causes cancer and heart disease.

2. Everyone knows that we must eat food **in order to** live.
   a. What information follows **in order to**?
      1. the reason
      2. the result
      3. the cause
   b. Complete the following sentence correctly.

      Cindy went to the supermarket in order to
      1. walk to the store
      2. learn how to cook
      3. buy some food

3. What type of food is healthy? What **kind** of food can be bad for our health?

   In these sentences, which word is a synonym of **kind**?

   _____TYPE_____

4. In 1956, the **USDA** described **four basic food groups**: meat (meat, fish, chicken, etc.), dairy (cheese, butter, etc.), grains (bread, cereals, rice, etc.), and fruit and vegetables. The USDA suggested how much of each food group was healthy to eat **daily**.
   a. Look at line 3 of the passage. What is the USDA?

      _____

   b. How do you know?

      _____

   c. This information is called a

      _____footnote_____

    d.   What are the four basic food groups? Give examples of each group.

       1.   *meat: meat, fish, chicken*

       2.   *dairy: milk, cheese, butter*

       3.   *grain: bread, cereals, rice*

       4.   *fruit and vegetables.*

    e.   What does **daily** mean?

       1.   every day
       2.   a lot of
       3.   a little of

5. Americans eat a lot of meat and only a small amount of grains, fruit, and vegetables. In Japan, **in contrast**, people eat large amounts of grains and very little meat. The Japanese also have very low rates of cancer and heart disease. **In fact**, the Japanese live longer than **anyone else** in the world.

    a.   What information follows **in contrast**?

       1.   a similar idea
       2.   an opposite idea
       3.   the same idea

    b.   What information follows **in fact**?

       1.   more information about the same idea
       2.   contrasting information about the same idea
       3.   surprising information about the same idea

    c.   What does **anyone else** mean?

       1.   all other people
       2.   some other people
       3.   most other people

6. **Unfortunately**, when Japanese people move to the United States, their rates of heart disease and cancer increase **as** their diet changes. **Moreover**, as hamburgers, ice cream, and other high-fat foods become popular in Japan, the rates of heart disease and cancer increase **there**, too.

    a.   What follows **unfortunately**?

       1.   something lucky
       2.   something bad
       3.   something false

    b.   What does **as** mean?

       1.   when
       2.   so
       3.   and

   c. What does **moreover** mean?
  1. however
  2. also ⁓
  3. then

   d. What are some examples of high-fat foods?

                 _hamburgers and ice cream._

   e. Where does **there** refer to?
  1. in the United States
  2. in Cuba
  3. in Japan ⁓

7. People are also eating more meat and dairy products in other countries **such as** Cuba, Mauritius, and Hungary. **Not surprisingly**, the disease rates in these countries are increasing along with the change in diet. **Consequently**, doctors everywhere advise people to eat more grains, fruit, and vegetables, and to eat less meat and fewer dairy products.

   a. What does **such as** mean?
  1. for example
  2. instead of
  3. except in

   b. What information follows **not surprisingly**?
  1. information that is hard to believe
  2. information that is not true
  3. information that is easy to believe

   c. What does **consequently** mean?
  1. in addition
  2. as a result
  3. in fact

8. A healthy diet is important for children **as well as** adults.
   a. This sentence means that a healthy diet
  1. is more important for children than it is for adults
  2. is more important for adults than it is for children
  3. is equally important for both adults and children

   b. **As well as** means
  1. and also
  2. but not
  3. instead of

9. When adults have poor eating habits, their children usually do, too. **After all**, children eat the same way as their parents.
   a. The first sentence means that
      1. the children usually have better eating habits
      2. the children also have poor eating habits  ⁄
   b. Read the second sentence again. Then read the following sentence and complete it correctly.

   John speaks Spanish fluently. After all,
      1. he lived in Venezuela for 15 years  ⁄
      2. he reads many books about South America

10. Most doctors agree that fruit and vegetables can actually **prevent** many different diseases. **On the other hand**, animal fat can **cause** disease.
    a. What is the connection between **prevent** and **cause**?
       1. They have similar meanings.
       2. They have opposite meanings.  ⁄
    b. What does **prevent** mean?
       1. to keep from happening  ⁄
       2. to make happen
    c. What information follows **on the other hand**?
       1. a similar idea
       2. an example of the idea
       3. an opposite idea  ⁄
    d. Read the following sentences. Complete the second sentence correctly.

    I may visit many different places on my vacation. On the other hand,
       1. I may go to museums, zoos, parks and beaches
       2. I may stay at home and relax  ⁄

## D. Word Forms

### Part 1

In English, verbs change to nouns in several ways. Some verbs become nouns by adding the suffix -*ment*, for example, *announce* (v.), *announcement* (n.).

Complete each sentence with the correct form of the words on the left. **Write all the verbs in the simple present tense. They may be affirmative or negative. The nouns may be singular or plural.**

improve (v.)
improvement (n.)

1. Manufacturers have made many _improvements_ in computers in the last ten years. For example, they are smaller, faster, and more dependable. Now manufacturers are trying to _improve_ their complexity.

agree (v.)
agreement (n.)

2. Some people are vegetarians. They think that all meat is bad, but Fay _doesn't agree_. She thinks that meat is good to eat occasionally. However, she is in _____ with the idea that vegetables and fruit are very healthy.

encourage (v.)
encouragement (n.)

3. Jason is my best friend. He always _encourages_ me when I have a difficult problem. In fact, his _____ has helped me succeed many times.

develop (v.)
development (n.)

4. Scientists are working to _develop_ a cure for all kinds of cancer. The _____ of a cure will be welcome all around the world.

enjoy (v.)
enjoyment (n.)

5. I _do not enjoy_ going to the movies alone. I prefer going with a friend. Sharing a good movie adds to my _____ .

## Part 2

In English, the noun form and the verb form of some word are the same, for example, *move* (v.), *move* (n.).

Complete each sentence with the correct form of the word on the left. In addition, indicate whether you are using the verb (v.) or the noun (n.) form of each word. **Write all the verbs in the simple present tense. They may be affirmative or negative. The nouns may be singular or plural.**

research

1. Dr. Johnson *research* [*doesn't*] cures for cancer. She
   (v., n.)

   does all her _____ on heart disease.
   (v., n.)

increase

2. During the summer, the temperature *increases*
   (v., n.)

   about 30° F. This significant _____ in tem-
   (v., n.)

   perature makes many people uncomfortable.

taste

3. I like the sweet _____ of fruit such as
   (v., n.)

   cherries and pears. Lemons *don't taste* sweet.
   (v., n.)

   They are very sour.

cause

4. There are many *causes* of cancer. For exam-
   (v., n.)

   ple, sometimes exposure to the sun _____ *causes*
   (v., n.)

   skin cancer.

change

5. In some areas of the world, there are four

   *changes* in season. However, in other coun-
   (v., n.)

   tries, the weather *change* at all. It is the
   (v., n.)

   same all year. There is only one season.

---

## E. Vocabulary in Context

agree (v.)  *8*        describe (v.) *3*    suggestion (n.) *6*
as a result  *5*       disease (n.) *9*     type (adj.) *7*
because of             prevent (v.) *4*     unfortunately (adv.) *2*
confused (adj.) *1*

Read each sentence below. Fill in each space with the correct word from the list above. Use each word only once.

1.  Your directions are not clear. I'm very _____ , and I'm afraid of getting lost.

2.  Mary and Tom went on a picnic in the park. _____ , they stayed out in the sun too long and became sunburned.

3.  I have just moved into a new apartment. I'll _____ it to you. It's on the third floor, it has three large rooms and a big kitchen, and it gets the sunlight all day.

4.  Some people believe that it is possible to _____ colds by drinking a lot of orange juice every day.

5.  Emily lost her umbrella last week. _____ , she had to buy a new one.

6.  Leslie said, "Let's go to the Art Museum." Robert said, "That's a wonderful _____ !"

7.  I like to read mysteries and biographies. What _____ of books do you like to read?

8.  Michael thinks Italian food is delicious, and I _____ with him.

9.  Cancer is a very serious _____ .

10. Fred got a good job _____ his experience with computers.

## F. Follow-up Activities

1. Larry is a student at the State University. The following menu shows what he usually eats for breakfast, lunch and dinner. How can you change Larry's menu in order to make it healthier for him?

   **Breakfast**
   > two eggs
   > two slices of white bread with butter
   > one cup of coffee with cream and sugar

   **Lunch**
   > one large chocolate ice cream cone

   **Dinner**
   > one hamburger on a roll
   > one large order of French fries
   > an order of broccoli
   > lettuce and tomatoes

   **Late-night snack**
   > a bag of potato chips
   > an apple

2. Alone, or with one or more classmates, go to a fast food restaurant. Order a healthy meal. Report to the class on the meal you ate and why it was nutritious.

3. Alone, or with a student from your country, prepare a menu for a typical breakfast, lunch, and dinner in your country. Then talk to a student from another country, and show the student your menu. Explain why you think your diet is healthy; then ask the other student to explain why he or she thinks his/her diet is healthy. Compare your menu with the student's menu from a different country. Discuss which diet you both think is healthier.

## G. Topics for Discussion and Writing

1. Are there high rates of heart disease and cancer in your country? What do you think are some reasons for this?

2. Do you have children? What kind of food do you give them? Why? Do they enjoy the food? If you don't have children, imagine that you do. What kind of food do you give them? Why?

3. The reading passage discusses a healthy diet as a way to prevent disease. Work with a classmate. Make a list of other ways to prevent disease. Compare your list with your classmates' lists.

## H. Crossword Puzzle: A Healthy Diet for Everyone

### Across Clues

4. Study very carefully
5. As a result
7. The opposite of **yes**
9. The opposite of **on**
11. Also; furthermore
12. In good physical condition
13. Rice and cereals are
    _____ .
14. Keep from happening
17. The opposite of **down**
19. When we make many _____,
    we make things better.
20. The opposite of **no**
22. Illness; sickness
23. The opposite of **bottom**

### Down Clues

1. I am. She _____ .
2. Every day
3. Type
5. _____ is a very serious
   illness.
6. Unhappily
8. You have a choice: you can have
   either coffee _____ tea.
10. _____ and vegetables are
    very good for us to eat.
13. The are four basic food
    _____ .
15. Milk, butter, and ice cream are
    _____ products.
16. I am _____ . I don't
    understand what you said.
18. He is. We _____ .
21. Beef and chicken are types of
    _____ .
22. Everything we eat is part of our
    _____ .

## I. CLOZE Quiz

| | | |
|---|---|---|
| a lot of | large amounts of | too much |
| a small amount of | less | very little |
| fewer | more | very low rates of |
| high rates of | | |

Read the passage below. Fill in each space with one of the words or phrases listed above. You may use them more than once. **In addition, there may be more than one correct answer.**

As a result of years of research, we know that (1) _Too much_ animal fat is bad for our health. For example, Americans eat (2) _a lot of_ meat and only (3) _a small amount of_ grains, fruit, and vegetables. Because of their diet, they have (4) _high rates of_ cancer and heart disease. In Japan, in contrast, people eat (5) _a lot of_ grains and (6) _very little_ meat. The Japanese also have (7) _very low rates of_ cancer and heart disease. In fact, the Japanese live longer than anyone else in the world. Consequently, doctors everywhere advise people to eat (8) _more_ grains, fruit, and vegetables and (9) _less_ meat and (10) _fewer_ dairy products.

## Unit IV Discussion

We can do many things to have a healthy life. With a classmate or in a small group, discuss what you can do to have a healthy life.

# UNIT V

## The Earth's Resources and Dangers

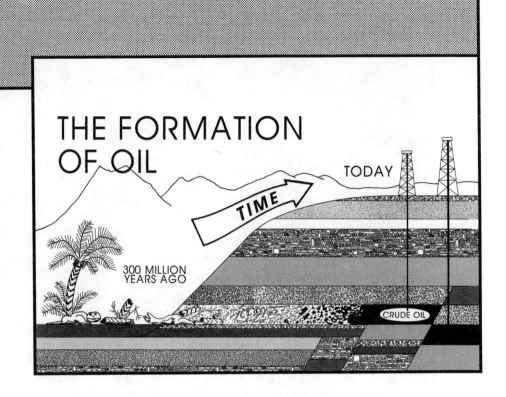

THE FORMATION
OF OIL

TODAY

TIME

300 MILLION
YEARS AGO

CRUDE OIL

# CHAPTER 9

## Oil: An Important World Resource

---

## Prereading Preparation

1. Look at the illustration on the left. How long does it take oil to form? Describe the process.
2. What are some uses of oil?

   _____   _____

   _____   _____

   _____   _____

3. What is a natural resource?
4. Does your country produce oil?
5. Name some countries that produce oil.

1　　In the early 1800s, Americans needed salt, so they drilled
2　wells to bring salty water to the surface. When the water evap-
3　orated in the sun, they had a supply of salt. Sometimes the
4　salty water was mixed with oil. The people were very disap-
5　pointed because they couldn't use the oil. However, circum-
6　stances began to change in the 1820s. In those days, people
7　used whale oil to light their lamps and to make candles.
8　Unfortunately, many whales were killed, and it was very diffi-
9　cult to find them, so whale oil became very expensive. People
10　needed another source of oil to light their homes. The oil that
11　came from the ground suddenly became useful. In 1859, in
12　Titusville, Pennsylvania, a man named Edwin Drake drilled
13　the first oil well, and started the American oil industry.
14　　Oil is usually called petroleum. Petroleum is very complex,
15　but it is made up of only two elements: carbon (C) and hydro-
16　gen (H). Together carbon and hydrogen are called hydrocar-
17　bons. Hydrocarbons are the remains of ancient plants and ani-

18  mals. These plants and animals lived and died millions of
19  years ago. When they died, they were covered by mud, and
20  bacteria broke down the organic remains. Over thousands of
21  years, more plants and animals died and were covered by
22  more mud. The weight of the upper layers and the heat from
23  the pressure eventually changed the mud into solid rock,
24  called sedimentary rock. It also changed the organic material
25  into oil and natural gas.
26      When petroleum first comes out of the ground, it is called
27  crude oil. This oil is impure. In other words, it is dirty, and
28  people need to clean it. When they clean, or refine, it, they
29  manufacture different products. They put the oil into a fur-
30  nace to heat it. The lightest part of the oil becomes natural
31  gas. We use natural gas to heat our homes and to cook with.
32  The heaviest part of the oil becomes asphalt. We use asphalt to
33  pave roads and parking lots. In between the natural gas and
34  the asphalt, this process produces gasoline, kerosene, heating
35  oil, and lubricating oil. We use gasoline to operate our cars.
36  We need lubricating oil to grease machines and other metal
37  objects with moving parts, for example, sewing machines.
38      Petroleum products are called petrochemicals. Many of
39  the products we see and use every day are petrochemicals, for
40  instance, synthetic rubber and synthetic fibers such as nylon,
41  Orlon, and Dacron. The detergent we use to wash dishes and
42  clean our clothes, the vitamins we take, and some of the drugs
43  that our doctors prescribe are petrochemicals. Plastic contain-
44  ers and toys, shampoo, lipstick, and hand lotion are petro-
45  chemicals, too. In fact, more than six thousand products we
46  buy and use are petrochemicals.

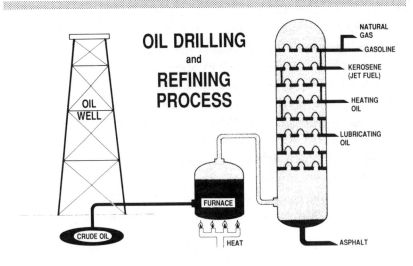

OIL DRILLING
and
REFINING
PROCESS

OIL WELL

FURNACE

CRUDE OIL

HEAT

NATURAL GAS
GASOLINE
KEROSENE (JET FUEL)
HEATING OIL
LUBRICATING OIL
ASPHALT

## A. Fact-Finding Exercise

Read the passage once. Then read the following statements. Check whether they are true (T) or false (F). If a statement is false, change the statement so that it is true. Then go back to the passage and find the line that supports your answer.

___✓ T   ___F   1. Before 1850, people used whale oil to light their homes.

_____

___ T   ___F   2. The American oil industry began in the early 1800s.

*It began in 1859*

___✓ T   ___F   3. **Petroleum** is another word for oil.

_____

___ T   ___F   4. Crude oil is ready to use.

*It's not ready to use. People need to clean it*

___✓ T   ___F   5. The lightest part of the oil becomes natural gas.

_____

___ T   ___F   6. We do not use petroleum products very often.

*We use petroleum products every day*

## B. Information Recall

Read the passage a second time. Then try to answer the following questions. Do not look back at the passage. Compare your answers with a classmate's answers.

1. a.   What did people use to light their homes before the oil industry began?

   *They used whale oil to light their lamps and to make candles*

   b.   Why did it become expensive?

   *because many whales were killed, and it was very difficult to find*

2. a.   What does the lightest part of the oil become?

   *It becomes natural gas*

   b.   What do we use it for?

   *we use it to heat our homes and to cook with*

3. a.   What does the heaviest part of the oil become?

_It becomes asphalt_

  b.   What do we use it for?

_we use it to pave roads and parking lots._

4.   What are some petrochemical products that we use every day?

_Synthetic rubber and synthetic fibers, detergent, vitamins, drugs, plastic containers, toys, shampoo, lipstick and hand lotion._

## C. Reading Analysis

Read each question carefully. Either circle the letter of the correct answer, or write your answer in the space provided.

1.   What is the main idea of this passage?
  a.   Oil is dirty when it comes from the ground and needs to be cleaned.
  b.   Both oil and natural gas are natural resources.
  c.   Oil is an important natural resource that has many everyday uses.

2.   In **the early 1800s**, Americans drilled wells.

  **The early 1800s** refers to the years
  a.   1800–1850
  b.   1800–1830
  c.   1820–1850

3.   People couldn't use the oil that was mixed with the salty water. However, **circumstances** began to change in the 1820s. **In those days**, people used whale oil to light their homes. Unfortunately, many **whales** were killed, and it was very difficult to find them, so whale oil became very expensive. People needed another source of oil to light their homes.
  a.   What does **circumstances** mean?
    1.   prices
    2.   whales
    3.   conditions
  b.   What were the **circumstances** that changed?
    1.   Oil was mixed in the salty water, and it was difficult to get the oil out of the water.
    2.   Whale oil was expensive because it was hard to find whales, so people wanted a new, cheap kind of oil.

   c.  In these sentences, what does **in those days** refer to?
     1.  1820–1825
     2.  1826–1829
     _3.  1820–1829

4. In 1859, in **Titusville**, Pennsylvania, a man named Edwin Drake drilled the first oil well.

   What is **Titusville**?
   a.  a state in the United States
  b.  a city in Pennsylvania
   c.  a country in North America

5. Hydrocarbons are the **remains** of ancient plants and animals that lived millions of years ago. When these plants and animals died, bacteria broke down the **organic** remains.
   a.  In these sentences, **remains** are
     1.  the places where the dead animals and plants lived
    2.  the bodies of the animals and plants
   b.  The adjective **organic** means
    1.  any living or dead plants or animals
     2.  only living plants and animals

6. When the oil comes out of the ground, it is **impure. In other words**, it is dirty, and people need to clean it.
   a.  What does **impure** mean?
     1.  oil
    2.  dirty
     3.  from the ground
   b.  What type of information follows the phrase **in other words**?
     1.  an example
     2.  additional information
    3.  the same information in different words

7. People put the oil into a **furnace** to heat it. Many homes and apartment buildings have **furnaces**. People use furnaces to
   a.  supply fresh air for buildings
   b.  keep the air in buildings clean
  c.  supply heat for buildings during cold weather

8. Many of the products we see and use every day are petrochemicals, **for instance**, synthetic rubber and synthetic fibers **such as** nylon, Orlon, and Dacron.
   a. Which phrase is a synonym of **for instance**?
      1. in addition
      2. for example
      3. in contrast
   b. What are nylon, Orlon, and Dacron?

      _____ synthetic fibers _____
   c. How do you know?

      _____ such as _____
   d. **Synthetic** means
      1. man-made
      2. natural
   e. Cotton, wool, silk, and linen are also fibers. Are they also synthetic fibers, or are they natural fibers?

      _____ they are natural fibers _____

9. Plastic containers and toys, shampoo, lipstick, and hand lotion are petrochemicals, too. **In fact**, more than six thousand products we buy and use are petrochemicals.
   a. What does **in fact** mean?
      1. really
      2. however
      3. also
   b. Complete the following sentence with the appropriate choice.

      Yesterday was a very cold day. In fact,
      1. I had to wear a heavy coat
      2. it snowed all day long
      3. the temperature was 10° F below zero
   c. What kind of information follows **in fact**?
      1. the same information as the information before it, but in different words
      2. specific information to emphasize the information before it
      3. new information about a different topic than the information before it

## D. Word Forms

### Part 1

In English, verbs change to nouns in several ways. Some verbs become nouns by adding the suffix *-tion*, for example, *create* (v.), *creation* (n.). If the word ends in *-e*, drop the *-e* before adding *-tion*. Furthermore, sometimes the spelling of the word changes.

Complete each sentence with the correct form of the words on the left. **Write all the verbs in the simple present tense. They may be affirmative or negative. The nouns may be singular or plural.**

evaporate (v.)

evaporation (n.)

1.  The process of ＿＿＿＿＿ causes water to change from a liquid to a gas. Heat from the sun or from a radiator usually _evaporates_ water very quickly.

lubricate (v.)

lubrication (n.)

2.  Monica takes care of her bicycle, so she carefully _lubricates_ the gears and the chain every month. She uses a good-quality oil for proper ＿＿＿＿＿ .

produce (v.)

production (n.)

3.  Australia _produce_ very much petroleum or natural gas. In fact, Australia's yearly ＿＿＿＿＿ of oil and gas is the lowest in the world.

prescribe (v.)

prescription (n.)

4.  Doctors are the only people who can write out ＿＿＿＿＿ for certain drugs that can be dangerous. However, doctors _prescribe_ basic drugs such as aspirin. We can buy them easily.

add (v.)

addition (n.)

5.  Bill and Arthur always _add_ the figures on their check when they go to a restaurant. Sometimes the waiter makes mistakes when he does his ＿＿＿＿＿ , so Bill and Arthur like to make sure the total is correct.

## Part 2

In English, the noun form and the verb form of some words are the same, for example, *drill* (v.), *drill* (n.).

Complete each sentence with the correct form of the word on the left. In addition, indicate whether you are using the verb (v.) or the noun (n.) form of each word. **Write all the verbs in the simple present tense. They may be affirmative or negative. The nouns may be singular or plural.**

supply

1. Many countries now _____ the world with
   (v., n.)

   natural gas and oil, but these reserves are limited.

   At some time in the next one hundred years, the

   world's entire _____ will end, and all
   (v., n.)

   countries will need other sources of energy.

grease

2. There are many different types of _____ for
   (v., n.)

   various purposes. For example, whenever Fred

   ___*greases*___ his car, he uses different lubricants for
   (v., n.)

   different parts of his car.

light

3. Chris has many bright _____ around the
   (v., n.)

   outside of his house. He usually ___*doesn't light*___
   (v., n.)

   them all when he is home. He only turns them on

   when he is away, to frighten away robbers.

heat

4. In many countries of the world, people ___*don't heat*___
   (v., n.)

   their homes with oil or gas. They use wood or coal

   instead. The amount of _____ that a house
   (v., n.)

   gets is usually controlled with an instrument called

   a thermostat.

process

5. Numerous _____ are involved in the oil-
   (v., n.)

   refining industry. However, most oil companies

   _____ crude oil in the same way.
   (v., n.)    *drop.*

## E. Vocabulary in Context

complex (adj.) 6    material (n.) 2    refine (v.)
impure (adj.) 5    mix (v.) 9    source (n.) 7
in fact 4    organic (adj.) 8    unfortunately (adv.) 3
in other words

Read each sentence below. Fill in each space with the correct word from the list above. Use each word only once.

1. When sugar cane is cut down, factories ___refine___ it to clean it and prepare it for sale.

2. Nylon is a very strong _____, so clothing and parachutes are made of nylon.

3. Amanda studied hard for her math test. _____, she was sick the day of the test, so she didn't do very well.

4. Thomas comes from a large family. _____, he has six brothers and five sisters!

5. The water in many lakes and rivers is _____. As a result, it needs to be cleaned before people can drink it.

6. A car is a very _____ machine. However, a bicycle is a very simple machine.

7. The sun is a powerful _____ of light and heat.

8. Grass and leaves are _____, but rocks and glass are not.

9. If you _____ blue and yellow, you will get the color green.

10. Mario is a matriculated undergraduate student. _____, he is attending college in order to graduate and get a bachelor's degree.

## F. Follow-up Activities

1. Compare life today with life 150 years ago, before people used petroleum. What petroleum products do people use today? What did people use 150 years ago in place of these products?

| **Today** | **150 Years Ago** |
|---|---|
| a. _____ | homemade soap |
| b. gasoline-powered cars | _____ |
| c. electricity for lighting | _____ |
| d. oil and gas for home heating | _____ |
| e. _____ | stones to pave roads |
| f. _____ | natural rubber |
| g. nylon, Orlon, Dacron for clothes | _____ |

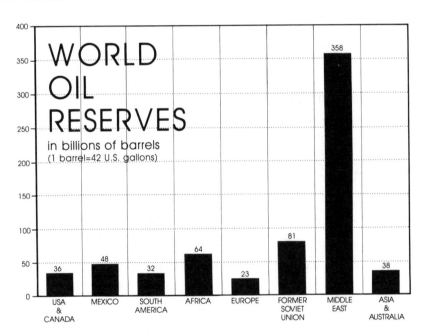

2. Refer to the WORLD OIL RESERVES BAR GRAPH above. Write the answers to the following questions.

   a.  Which country or area has the largest oil reserves in the world?

   _____

   b.  Which country or area has the smallest oil reserves in the world?

   _____

   c.  Which country or area has the second largest oil reserves in the world?

   _____

    d.  Which one of the following statements is true?
1. The Middle East has smaller oil reserves than all the other countries and areas combined.
2. The Middle East has the same amount of oil reserves as all the other countries and areas combined.
3. The Middle East has bigger oil reserves than all the other countries and areas combined.

## G. Topics for Discussion and Writing

1. Think about people's lives at home, at work, at school, etc. Describe how oil makes life easier for people.
2. The reading passage explains the process of changing oil into different products. Think of another process where something is changed into a useful product. Describe it and the process, for example, how people change wood into paper.
3. There are many other scientific advances that make life better or easier for us. Work with a classmate, and make a list. Then select one advance and describe it.
4. Imagine that there is no more oil in the world. Describe a day in your life without oil.

## H. Crossword Puzzle: Oil

**Across Clues**

1. One, _____ , three, four
4. When oil comes out of the ground, it is _____ , or dirty.
6. The opposite of **out**
7. Oil is a mixture of two elements. Together, they are called _____ .
13. We use _____ to pave our highways and parking lots. It is black and heavy oil.
15. We use _____ to clean our clothes and to wash our dishes.
17. Natural gas is the _____ part of processed oil. Gasoline is heavier.
19. He, _____ , it
20. People hunted these animals to use their oil in lamps.
22. The opposite of **yes**
23. Another word for **oil**

**Down Clues**

2. We _____ our clothes and our dishes with detergent.
3. A _____ is an enclosed space used to produce a lot of heat.
5. It takes _____ of years for petroleum to form.
8. The opposite of **off**
9. My uncle and _____ wear clothes made of nylon, Orlon, and Dacron.
10. Oil is measured in _____ . One of them equals 42 U.S. gallons.
11. The opposite of **down**
12. _____ means man-made.
14. Gasoline, heating oil, and _____ are made from oil.
16. We _____ the moving parts of machines in order to lubricate them.
18. The opposite of **from**

24. We use different types of oil in our _____ , or automobiles.
25. A type of rock that is formed in layers, one on top of the other.

21. When we clean oil, we _____ it.
23. In the _____, people did not have a use for oil. Today we cannot live without it.
26. The opposite of **bottom**
27. The opposite of **no**

## I. CLOZE Quiz

is       are       was       were

Read the passage below. Fill in each space with a form of *be* listed above. You may use the words more than once.

   In the early 1800s, people used whale oil to light their lamps and to make candles. Unfortunately, whale oil (1) _____ very expensive, and people needed another source of oil to light their homes. Suddenly, the oil that came from the ground (2) _____ useful. Oil (3) _____ usually called petroleum. Petroleum (4) _____ very complex, but it (5) _____ made up of only two elements: carbon (C) and hydrogen (H). Together carbon and hydrogen (6) _____ called hydrocarbons. Hydrocarbons (7) _____ the remains of ancient plants and animals. These plants and animals lived and died millions of years ago. When they died, they (8) _____ covered by mud, and bacteria broke down the organic remains. Over thousands of years, more plants and animals died and (9) _____ covered by more mud.

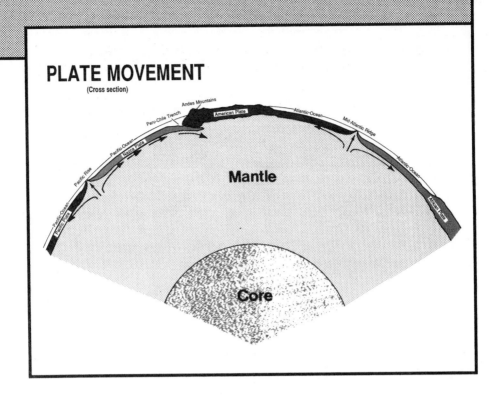

## PLATE MOVEMENT
(Cross section)

# CHAPTER 10

# Earthquakes: What Are They and How Do They Happen?

---

## Prereading Preparation

1. Look at the illustration on the left. What does it show? What are continents? Do all the continents move in the same direction?
2. What is an earthquake?
3. What happens during an earthquake?
4. Why are earthquakes dangerous?
5. Can scientists predict earthquakes? Why is this important?
6. Where in the world do earthquakes occur? Do earthquakes occur in your country?

---

1  Earthquake! People all around the world fear earthquakes.
2  However, many people do not understand them very well.
3  To understand what causes earthquakes, we need to
4  understand the nature of the Earth and the changes that are
5  slowly taking place in the Earth's crust, or surface. The crust is
6  made of rock. The crust covers the Earth, but it is not in one
7  piece. It is broken into a number of large pieces called plates.
8  These plates are always moving because they lie on top of liq-
9  uid rock. They slide over the hot, melted rock. The continents
10 ride on top of the plates and move with them. The plates move
11 very slowly, usually at a rate of a few inches per year.
12  The plates move in different directions. The difference in
13 motion causes the rocks to break. This is an earthquake.
14 Earthquakes happen in different ways. In some areas of the
15 Earth, the plates move apart. This happens in the middle of

16  the Atlantic Ocean. The plates are sliding past one another in
17  other regions of the world, for example, at the San Andreas
18  fault zone in California. In other places, plates push directly
19  against each other, and one plate moves downward under the
20  other plate. For example, this happens off the western coasts
21  of South and Central America and off the coast of Japan.
22      Earthquakes also take place inside of plates throughout
23  the world. For instance, China is being squeezed in two direc-
24  tions, from the east by the Pacific plate and from the south by
25  the India-Australia plate.
26      Many scientists are trying to predict earthquakes, but
27  these predictions are very uncertain. Scientists cannot predict
28  the exact location, time, or intensity of an earthquake.
29  Furthermore, the predicted earthquake may not take place
30  at all. As a result, they do not think it is a useful idea to
31  announce that an earthquake will take place on a specific day.
32  Instead, people are trying to design structures such as build-
33  ings, dams, and bridges that can resist earthquakes. They are
34  also trying to teach the public how to prepare for and survive
35  earthquakes.

---

## A. Fact-Finding Exercise

Read the passage once. Then read the following statements. Check whether
they are true (T) or false (F). If a statement is false, change the statement so
that it is true. Then go back to the passage and find the line that supports
your answer.

____ T  ✓ F  1. The crust covers the earth in one piece.

    *It is broken into many pieces*

✓ T  ____ F  2. The continents of the world are above the plates.

_____

____ T  ✓ F  3. All the plates move in one direction.

    *the plates move in several different direction*

✓ T  ____ F  4. Sometimes earthquakes happen when the plates
move apart.

_____

____ T  ✓ F  5. Scientists know when and where an earthquake will
happen in the future.

    *do not*

    *they can not predict earthquakes*

## B. Information Recall

Read the passage a second time. Then try to answer the following questions. Do not look back at the passage. Compare your answers with a classmate's answers.

1. Describe the crust of the earth.

   _____

   _____

2. a.  How do earthquakes happen?

   _____

   b.  How many different ways can earthquakes happen?

   _____

   c.  Describe the different ways earthquakes can happen.

   _____

   _____

   _____

   _____

3. a.  Can scientists predict exactly when and where earthquakes will happen?

   _____

   b.  How can people prepare for earthquakes?

   _____

## C. Reading Analysis

Read each question carefully. Either circle the letter of the correct answer, or write your answer in the space provided.

1. What is the main idea of this passage?
   - a.  Earthquakes happen in different ways in different parts of the Earth.
   - b.  Earthquakes kill many people and cause a lot of damage.
   - c.  It is difficult to predict when an earthquake will happen.

2. People all around the world fear earthquakes. **However**, many people do not understand them very well.
   a. These sentences mean that
      1. many people are afraid of earthquakes, but they do not know very much about them
      2. many people are afraid of earthquakes because they do not know very much about them
   b. **However** means
      1. because
      2. but
      3. and

3. We need to understand the changes that are slowly taking place in the Earth's **crust**, or surface.

   In this sentence, which word is a synonym of **crust**?

   _Surface_

4. The crust is broken into many large pieces called plates. These plates are always moving because they lie on top of **liquid rock**. They slide over the hot, melted rock. The continents ride on top of the plates and move with them.

   In this paragraph, which words describe what **liquid rock** is like?

   _hot, melted rock_

5. In some **areas** of the Earth, the plates move apart. The plates are sliding past one another in other regions of the world, for example, at the San Andreas fault zone in California.

   In these sentences, which words are synonyms of **area**?

   _region, zone_

6. Plates push directly against each other, and one plate moves downward under another plate. **For example**, this happens off the western coasts of South and Central America. Earthquakes also take place inside of plates. For instance, China is being squeezed from the east by the Pacific plate and from the south by the India-Australia plate.
   a. In this paragraph, which phrase is a synonym of **example**?

   _For instance_

   b. These two phrases introduce
      1. explanations
      2. results
      3. examples

7. Many scientists are trying to **predict** earthquakes, but these **predictions** are very uncertain. Scientists cannot **predict** the exact location, time, or intensity of an earthquake. **Furthermore**, the predicted earthquake may not take place at all.
   a.  **Predict** means
       1.  stop something from happening
       2.  tell something will happen before it happens
       3.  understand something by reading about it
   b.  What information comes after **furthermore**?
       1.  more information about the same subject
       2.  the same information in different words
       3.  the result of the information before **furthermore**

8. Many scientists are trying to predict earthquakes, but these predictions are very uncertain. The predicted earthquake may not take place at all. **As a result**, they do not think it is a useful idea to announce that an earthquake will take place on a specific day.
   a.  Complete the following sentence correctly.

       Elizabeth read several interesting books about earthquakes. As a result,
       1.  she became a better reader
       2.  she decided to live in California
       3.  she learned many new facts about earthquakes
   b.  **As a result** means
       1.  moreover
       2.  consequently
       3.  however

9. People are trying to design structures **such as** buildings, dams, and bridges that can **resist** earthquakes.
   a.  Which one of the following sentences does **such as** belong in?
       1.  Ann bought many vegetables _____ potatoes, carrots, and broccoli.
       2.  Ann bought many vegetables _____ fruit, cereal, and milk.
       3.  Ann bought many vegetables _____ boil, bake, and fry.
   b.  **Such as** means
       1.  in addition
       2.  in contrast
       3.  for example

c.   Some buildings can **resist** earthquakes. If there is an earthquake, these buildings
1.   will be unsafe and will fall down
2.   will be safe and will not fall down

---

## D. Word Forms

### Part 1

In English, verbs change to nouns in several ways. Some verbs become nouns by adding the suffix *-ment*, for example, *improve* (v.), *improvement* (n.).
Complete each sentence with the correct form of the words on the left. **Write all the verbs in the simple present tense. They may be affirmative or negative. The nouns may be singular or plural.**

move (v.)
movement (n.)

1.   The continents ___move___ on plates on the Earth's crust. We don't notice this _____ because it is very slow.

place (v.)
placement (n.)

2.   Schools usually ___place___ new students in different English classes depending on their English abilities. The students' _____ depends on the scores they get on an English test.

announce (v.)
announcement (n.)

3.   Television stations interrupt programs to make important _____ as soon as they receive the news. However, they generally ___do not___ small news items until the regular news programs.

arrange (v.)
arrangement (n.)

4.   Cary is a caterer. He organizes parties for individuals. However, he ___does not___ parties for organizations. Customers are always happy with Cary's ___re.___ for their parties.

require (v.)
requirement (n.)

5.   Most American colleges have an English _____ for foreign students. For instance, many colleges ___require___ a TOEFL score of 500 or higher.

## Part 2

In English, the noun form and the verb form of some words are the same, for example, *cover* (v.), *cover* (n.).

    Complete each sentence with the correct form of the word on the left. In addition, indicate whether you are using the verb (v.) or the noun (n.) form of each word. **Write all the verbs in the simple present tense. They may be affirmative or negative. The nouns may be singular or plural.**

fear

1. Tom has a terrible _____ of airplanes.
                                    (v., n.)

    Tom _____ airplanes so much that he
            (v., n.)
    never even goes to airports.

change

2. People need to make many _____
                                      (v., n.)

    when they move to another country. However,

    they _*do not*_ everything in their lives!
        (v., n.)

ride

3. When it rains, Kathy and Blaise _____
                                      (v., n.)

    the train to work. It is a very long _____
                                    (v., n.)

    so they read the newspaper to make time pass more

    quickly.

cause

4. Earthquakes of high intensity _____
                                      (v., n.)

    a lot of damage to buildings, roads, and bridges.

    However, the main _*causes*_ of death
                          (v., n.)
    from earthquakes is falling buildings.

design

5. Eve has a book full of her own _____
                                      (v., n.)

    for clothes. She _*does not*_ sports or casual
              (v., n.)

    clothes, however. She only creates formal clothes.

---

## E. Vocabulary in Context

apart (adv.) 5     3however     7resist (v.)
downward (adv.)     predict (v.) 1    structures (n.) 4
for example 6     8 regions (n.)    2throughout (prep.)
9 furthermore (adv.) Thêm nữa

Read each sentence below. Fill in each space with the correct word from the list above. Use each word only once.

1. Weathermen can usually _____ rain and snowstorms correctly.

2. Helen wants to drive _____ the United States. She plans to see all the states in three months!

3. Harry wants to go to the movies tonight. _____ , he has to study for a mathematics test tomorrow.

4. Dams are very big _____ . They are built to hold a great deal of water and to produce electricity.

5. Jane took the clock _____ to see how it worked, but she doesn't know how to put it back together.

6. Earthquakes can damage many utilities, _____ gas lines, electrical lines, and water pipes.

7. Most new buildings in Japan _____ earthquakes because they are carefully designed.

8. Siberia is one of the coldest _____ in the world.

9. David needs clothes. He has to buy shirts, sweaters, and pants. _____ , he needs shoes and a new coat.

10. The elevator was on the tenth floor. It moved _____ to the first floor when Fred pushed the button.

## F. Follow-up Activities

1. A seismograph is an instrument that scientists use to locate and record earthquakes. Scientists measure the energy, or intensity, of earthquakes with a Richter scale. The Richter scale measures the intensity of earthquakes on a scale of 1 to 10.

### Recent Earthquakes Around the World

| Date | Location | Intensity on Richter Scale | Number of Deaths |
|------|----------|----------------------------|------------------|
| 1. 5/70 | Peru | 7.8 | 67,000 |
| 2. 9/73 | Yokohama, Japan | 8.3 | 200,000 |
| 3. 2/76 | Guatemala | 7.5 | 23,000 |
| 4. 6/76 | New Guinea | 7.1 | 6,000 |
| 5. 7/76 | Tangshan, China | 7.8 | 243,000 |
| 6. 8/76 | The Philippines | 8.0 | 6,500 |
| 7. 10/80 | Algeria | 7.3 | 5,000 |
| 8. 11/80 | Southern Italy | 7.0 | 3,100 |
| 9. 10/83 | Turkey | 6.9 | 2,000 |
| 10. 9/85 | Mexico City, Mexico | 8.1 | 9,000 |
| 11. 12/88 | Armenia | 6.8 | 55,000 |
| 12. 10/89 | California, U.S.A. | 6.9 | 59 |
| 13. 6/90 | Northern Iran | 7.7 | 35,000 |
| 14. 2/91 | Pakistan | 6.8 | 700 |

Read the list of earthquakes in the chart. Then mark the location of each earthquake on the map. Write the number next to the star on the map that indicates the location of the earthquake.

WORLD
EARTHQUAKE
SITES

2. a.  Read the following checklist for home safety during an earthquake.
     1.  Make sure that hanging lights are not above beds.
     2.  Make sure that beds are not right below heavy mirrors.
     3.  Make sure that beds are not right below framed pictures.
     4.  Make sure that beds are not right below shelves with lots of things that can fall.
     5.  Make sure that beds are not next to large windows.
     6.  Take all heavy objects off high shelves.
     7.  Take all breakable things off high shelves.
     8.  Make sure that heavy mirrors are well fastened to walls.
     9.  Make sure that heavy pictures are well fastened to walls.
     10. Make sure that air conditioners are well supported in windows.
   b.  Look at the photograph of the bedroom. Refer to your checklist. In pairs or small groups, decide how to make the bedroom safer in an earthquake. When you are finished, compare your safer bedroom with another group's bedroom.

3. It is important to know what to do during an earthquake. Read the following list. In pairs, decide what to do and what not to do during an earthquake. When you finish, compare your list with the list of another pair of students. Be prepared to give reasons for your decisions.

___Yes ___No 1. Stay calm and don't do anything to upset other people.

___Yes ___No 2. Run to other rooms, and shout "Earthquake! Earthquake!"

___Yes ___No 3. If you are indoors, get under a desk or a table, if possible.

___Yes ___No 4. If you are in a high building, take the elevator to the first floor.

___Yes ___No 5. If you are in a building, do not run outside. Falling objects are a danger.

___Yes ___No 6. If you are outside near a building, stand in a doorway.

___Yes ___No 7. If you are outside, but not near a building, try to get into an open area away from buildings and power lines.

___Yes ___No 8. If you are in a car, continue driving to get as far away from the earthquake as possible.

___Yes ___No 9. If the electrical power lines and gas lines break, use matches and candles for light.

___Yes ___No 10. If you are in an empty room with no desk or table, stand in a doorway.

## G. Topics for Discussion and Writing

1. Imagine that an earthquake took place where you live. Describe the experience. What happened immediately before the earthquake? What happened during the earthquake? What happened after the earthquake? What did you think about? How did you feel?

2. If you know someone who experienced an earthquake, interview that person. Then write a composition describing the person's experience.

3. Form a team of three. An earthquake took place an hour ago. Your team must organize a rescue in your school building. Decide what you have to do. List these actions in their order of importance. Assign responsibilities to each member of the team. Have each team member write a composition describing his or her plan of action.

4. Imagine that you are a teacher. Prepare a set of instructions for your students. Tell them what to do if an earthquake occurs.

## G. Crossword Puzzle: Earthquakes

### Across Clues

2. The opposite of **off**
3. Some areas of the Earth are moving closer together, but other areas are moving _____.
5. Sometimes plates _____ directly against each other as they move closer.
8. Tell about something before it happens
10. The San Andreas fault is in this state.
11. One, _____, three, four
12. The surface of the Earth
14. A synonym of **but**
15. China is being squeezed in two _____ : from the east and from the south.

### Down Clues

1. The Earth's crust is not in one piece. It is _____ into many large pieces.
2. Happen; take place
4. Stand up to; survive
5. Another word for **area** or **location**
6. Be afraid
7. Australia, Africa, Asia, Europe, Antarctica, North America, and South America are _____.
8. The Earth's crust is in many pieces called _____.
9. Earthquakes take place in Japan. They take place in China, _____.
13. When a plate moves under another plate, it moves _____ .

19. The area along the ocean is called the _____.
20. The Earth's plates move, and rock breaks up. This is an _____.
21. Another word for **area**
22. Sometimes plates _____, or move, past each other.
23. Many people do not want to _____ their homes. They want to stay.
24. The opposite of **quickly**
25. Educated, trained people who study biology, chemistry, geology, etc.

16. Earthquakes happen all over the world. They take place _____ the world.
17. Many structures such as dams, bridges, and _____ are built to stand up to earthquakes.
18. Another word for **area**
19. The Americas are divided into North America, _____ America, and South America.
24. He, _____, it

## I. CLOZE Quiz

a      an      the

Read the passage below. Fill in each space with one of the articles listed above. You may use the words more than once.

(1) ___THE___ Earth's crust is broken into (2) ___a___ number of large pieces called plates. (3) ___the___ continents ride on top of (4) ___the___ plates and move with them. (5) ___the___ plates move very slowly, usually at (6) ___a___ rate of about (7) ___an___ inch per year.

(8) ___the___ plates move in different directions. (9) ___the___ difference in motion causes the rocks to break. This is (10) ___an___ earthquake. (11) ___an___ earthquake happens in different ways. In some areas of (12) ___the___ Earth, (13) ___the___ plates move apart. This happens in (14) ___the___ middle of (15) ___the___ Atlantic Ocean. (16) ___the___ plates are sliding past one another in other regions of (17) ___the___ world, for example, at (18) ___the___ San Andreas fault zone in California. In other places, plates push directly against each other, and one plate moves downward under (19) ___the___ other plate. For example, this happens off (20) ___the___ western coasts of South and Central America and off the coast of Japan.

## Unit V Discussion

The Earth produces oil, which is very useful. The Earth also creates earthquakes, which are very destructive. Work with a classmate. Make a list of other things that the Earth produces that are very useful. Then make a list of other things that the Earth produces that are destructive. Explain your choices.

# UNIT VI

## International
## Scientists

# CHAPTER 11

# Alfred Nobel: A Man of Peace

---

## Prereading Preparation

1. Look at the photograph on the left. Whose picture is on the award? What is this award? Who can receive it?
2. Who was Alfred Nobel? What kind of man do you think he was?
3. What is dynamite? Who invented it?
4. What are some different uses of dynamite? What are some helpful uses? What are some destructive uses?

1　　The headline in the newspaper announced the death of
2　Alfred Nobel on April 13, 1888. The reporter called him a
3　salesman of death, "The Dynamite King," because he invented
4　the powerful explosive dynamite. In fact, Alfred Nobel's dyna-
5　mite business had made him a very rich man. The newspaper
6　story continued, giving Alfred Nobel's age, nationality, and
7　other information about his business. However, the words
8　"The Dynamite King" were all that the 55-year-old Swedish
9　man read.
10　　Alfred Nobel sadly put down the newspaper. No, he wasn't
11　dead—his brother Ludwig had died the day before, and the
12　French newspaper made a mistake. All the same, Alfred Nobel
13　was disturbed. Was this the way the world was going to
14　remember him? He did not like that idea at all. He had spent
15　his life working for peace in the world. He hated violence and
16　war. He had invented dynamite to *save* lives—lives that were
17　lost because other explosives were dangerous to use. He
18　wanted people to remember him as a man of peace.
19　　Alfred Nobel invented dynamite at a perfect moment in

20   time. Many countries were beginning to build railroads and
21   tunnels, and needed a safe, powerful explosive to construct
22   railroad tracks through mountains. People also needed dyna-
23   mite to blow up stone in order to construct buildings, dams,
24   and roads. Alfred Nobel invented dynamite for these peaceful
25   uses. Moreover, he believed that if all countries had the same
26   powerful weapons, they would see how impossible war was,
27   and wars would end. In fact, this was a popular idea of his day.

28      Nobel was very upset about the image that the world had
29   of him, but he did not know what to do about it. He thought
30   about his problem for years. He wanted to think of the best
31   way for people to use his fortune of nine million dollars after
32   his death. Then, in 1895, an adventurer named Salomon
33   August Andrée made plans for an expedition to reach the
34   North Pole. People all over the world were excited about
35   Andrée's journey. Nobel read about Andrée's plan, too, and had
36   an inspiration. He finally knew what to do with his fortune.
37   He wrote his Last Will and Testament.* In his will, he instruct-
38   ed people to use all his money for an annual award to honor
39   leaders of science, literature, and world peace. He stated that
40   these leaders could be men or women of any nationality.

41      Alfred Nobel died on December 10, 1896, at the age of 63.
42   He was unmarried, and had no children. People all over the
43   world wondered who was going to get Nobel's money. They
44   were amazed when they learned of Alfred Nobel's plan to
45   award annual prizes in the fields of physics, chemistry, medi-
46   cine, literature, and peace. The first Nobel prizes were award-
47   ed in 1901, and they very soon became the greatest honor that
48   a person could receive in these fields. In 1969, an award for
49   economics was added.

50      The report of Alfred Nobel's death had been a mistake, but
51   the decision that he made because of this error gave the world
52   the image he wanted. Alfred Nobel established the Nobel
53   prize, and the world thinks of him the way he wanted to be
54   remembered: Alfred Nobel, man of peace.

---

*Last Will and Testament: A legal paper that states how a person wants his
or her possessions to be distributed after his or her death.

## A. Fact-Finding Exercise

Read the passage once. Then read the following statements. Check whether they are true (T) or false (F). If a statement is false, change the statement so that it is true. Then go back to the passage and find the line that supports your answer.

____ T ____ F  1. Alfred Nobel wanted people to remember him as the "Dynamite King."
    *He did not want people to remember this way*

____ T ____ F  2. Alfred Nobel died in 1888.
    *He died in 1896. His brother died in 1888*

____ T ____ F  3. Alfred Nobel invented dynamite.
    _____

____ T ____ F  4. Alfred Nobel hated violence.
    _____

____ T ____ F  5. Only men can receive a Nobel prize.
    *Men and women can receive the Nobel prize*

____ T ____ F  6. In 1895, Salomon August Andrée received the first Nobel prize.
    *In 1895, Andrée planned an expedition to the North pol*

## B. Information Recall

Read the passage a second time. Then try to answer the following questions. Do not look back at the passage. Compare your answers with a classmate's answers.

1. When Alfred Nobel read the newspaper on April 13, 1888, why did he become upset?

   _____

   _____

2. How did Nobel become rich?

   _____

   _____

3. a. What were some uses of dynamite?

   _____

   _____

   b. Why did Nobel believe he invented dynamite at a perfect moment in time?

   _____

   _____

4. a. Did Nobel believe that dynamite could stop wars?

   _____

   _____

   b. Why, or why not?

   _____

   _____

5. How did Nobel decide what he wanted people to do with his fortune after his death?

   _____

   _____

6. What instructions did Nobel leave in his Last Will and Testament?

   _____

   _____

7.  Who can receive the Nobel prize, and in what categories?

_____

_____

8.  What image does the world have of Alfred Nobel?

_____

_____

## C. Reading Analysis

Read each question carefully. Either circle the letter of the correct answer, or write your answer in the space provided.

1.  What is the main idea of this passage?
    a.   Alfred Nobel wrote his will after Andrée went to the North Pole.
    b.   The Nobel prize is an internationally famous award.
    c.   Alfred Nobel was a peaceful man who gave the world a great prize.

2.  The newspaper story gave Alfred Nobel's age, nationality, and other information about his business. **However**, the words "The Dynamite King" were all that the 55-year-old Swedish man read.

    a.   What does **however** mean?
        1.   and
        2.   but
        3.   then
    b.   Complete the following sentence correctly.

        Robert wanted to go to the beach. However,
        1.   it rained, so he stayed home
        2.   he asked his friends to go with him
        3.   he brought his lunch and a big umbrella

3.  The French newspaper made a mistake about Nobel. Ludwig Nobel died, not Alfred Nobel. **All the same**, Alfred Nobel was disturbed.

    These sentences mean that
    a.   because the news was a mistake, Alfred was not upset any more
    b.   it did not matter that the news was a mistake, Alfred was still upset

4. The world was going to remember him as "The Dynamite King." Alfred Nobel did not like that idea **at all**.

   This sentence means that
   a.   he liked the idea a little
   b.   he liked the idea a lot
   c.   he did not like anything about the idea

5. Nobel invented dynamite to save lives—lives that were lost because other explosives were dangerous to use.

   What follows the dash (—)?
   a.   a contrast
   b.   an example
   c.   an explanation

6. Alfred Nobel invented dynamite for peaceful uses. **Moreover**, he believed that if all countries had the same powerful weapons, they would see how impossible war was, and wars would end. This was a popular idea of **his day**.

   a.   **Moreover** means
        1.   however
        2.   in addition
        3.   as a result
   b.   Complete the following sentence correctly.

        Robert needed to learn English because he wanted to go to college in the United States. Moreover,
        1.   he had to speak English to get a good job
        2.   he hated to study and was a poor student
   c.   **His day** refers to
        1.   the day Nobel invented dynamite
        2.   the year 1895
        3.   the time that he lived

7. Nobel wanted to think of the best way for people to use his **fortune** of nine million dollars after his death.

   What is a synonym of **fortune**?
   a.   will
   b.   inspiration
   c.   wealth

8. In 1895, Alfred Nobel wrote his **Last Will and Testament**. In his **will**, he instructed people to use all his money for an annual award.

   a.   Look at line 37 of the passage. What is a **Last Will and Testament**?

   _____

   _____

   b.   How do you know?

   _____

   c.   This information is called a

   _____

   d.   What does the word **will** refer to?

   _____

9. Alfred Nobel had a plan to award annual prizes in the **fields** of physics, chemistry, medicine, literature, and peace.

   a.   What does **fields** mean?

   ___Subjects ; areas of study_____

   b.   Give some examples of **fields**.

   ___physics, chemistry, medicine, literature_____

10. The report of Alfred Nobel's death was a **mistake**, but the decision that he made because of this error gave the world the image he wanted.

   In this sentence, which word is a synonym of **mistake**?

   ___error._____

---

# D. Word Forms

## Part 1

In English, verbs change to nouns in several ways. Some verbs become nouns by adding the suffix *-ion* or *-ation*, for example, *suggest* (v.), *suggestion* (n.). Be careful of spelling changes, for example, *combine* (v.), *combination* (n.).

Complete each sentence with the correct form of the words on the left. **Write all the verbs in the simple past tense. They may be affirmative or negative. The nouns may be singular or plural.**

instruct (v.) *huấn luyện*
instruction (n.)

1. The proctor of the examination ___instructed___ the students to write their answers in pen, to skip a line, and to put their names on the paper. The students followed her ___instructions___ carefully.

invent (v.) *phát minh*
invention (n.)

2. Thomas Edison, an American, ___invented___ more than one thousand things. His ___inventions___ include the phonograph and the light bulb.

construct (v.) *xây dựng*
construction (n.)

3. The company finished the ___construction___ of its new office building. It ___did not construct___ the building of steel. It built it with bricks and wood.

inspire (v.) *cảm hứng*
inspiration (n.)

4. When the general gave a speech to his soldiers, he ___inspired___ them. As a result of the general's ___inspiration___, the men won the difficult battle.

continue (v.)
continuation (n.)

5. When Jenny graduated high school, she ___did not continue___ her education immediately. She went to college several years later. The ___continuation___ of her education had to wait until she saved enough money to pay her tuition.

## Part 2

In English, verbs change to nouns in several ways. Some verbs become nouns by adding the suffix *-ment*, for example, *improve* (v.), *improvement* (n.).

Complete each sentence with the correct form of the words on the left. **Write all the verbs in the simple past tense. They may be affirmative or negative. The nouns may be singular or plural.**

announce (v.)

announcement (n.)

1. Carol and Simon _announced_ their engagement yesterday. They plan to get married in two months. Their happy _____ surprised their friends.

excite (v.)

excitement (n.)

2. Lloyd went to a baseball game yesterday, but the game _did not excite_ him at all. However, I think there is a lot of _____ in a baseball game.

amaze (v.)

amazement (n.)

3. The magician was very talented, and he _amazed_ the children with his wonderful tricks. He smiled at their look of _____ when he sawed a woman in half.

establish (v.)

establishment (n.)

4. The directors discussed the formal _____ of a law school at the university ten years ago. However, they _did not_ the law school until this year.

state (v.)

statement (n.)

5. The governor made a few _statements_ last night. In his speech, he _stated_ that he intended to run for reelection next year and that he planned to cut taxes.

---

# E. Vocabulary in Context

all the same ₅   nationality (n.) ₇   too (adv.) ₄
at all ₉            peaceful (adj.) ₃   upset (adj.) ₆
headline (n.) ₁    perfect (adj.) ₂    violence (n.) ₈
mistake (n.) ₁₀

Read each sentence below. Fill in each space with the correct word from the list above. Use each word only once.

1.  Ellen saw the _____ "Earthquake Strikes the West Coast" on the front page of the *Tribune* and bought it to read the terrible news.

2.  Philip got an A on his math test because it was _____ . It did not have any errors.

3.  Everyone agrees that the lake area is a very _____ place for a vacation. It is very quiet and restful.

4.  William wants to go to the movies tonight. I want to see a movie, _____ .

5.  The weatherman reported sunny weather for today. _____ , I am going to bring my umbrella to work.

6.  Linda became very _____ when she lost her job. She needs the money.

7.  Carlos is Peruvian; Hiro is Japanese. What _____ are you?

8.  Mahatma Gandhi wanted independence for his country, but he did not believe in _____ . He worked for the independence of India without fighting.

9.  The weather was extremely dry last month. It did not rain _____ . I hope it rains soon!

10. Dominick found a small _____ on the third page of his term paper. He wrote **unpossible** instead of **impossible**.

## F. Follow-up Activities

1. Work in groups of three or four. You are part of a committee that has to decide on a new category for the Nobel prize. Remember, the fields now are physics, chemistry, medicine/physiology, literature, peace, and economics. Discuss your reasons why you think a seventh prize is a good idea. Compare your ideas with your classmates, then take a vote to decide on the new category.

2. Work in groups of three or four. You are part of a committee that has to decide to eliminate one category from the Nobel prize awards. Discuss your reasons why you think this prize is no longer necessary or desirable. Discuss your reasons with the class. Take a vote to decide on which category to eliminate.

3. Go to the library. Ask the librarian for a book that contains all the Nobel prize winners (an almanac). Make a list of the Nobel prize winners from your country or another country that you are interested in. Write down the years the people received their prizes, and the fields they received the prizes in. Then choose one person and write about his or her achievement.

## G. Topics for Discussion and Writing

1. Pretend that you are wealthy. What do you want to happen to your property and money after you die? Write instructions.

2. Write a composition describing how you want people to remember you.

3. Nominate a famous person for a Nobel prize in one of the six categories. Describe the person, and explain why you believe he or she deserves a Nobel prize in that field.

4. Go to the library. Use an almanac to find the list of all the Nobel prize winners. Select a Nobel prize winner from any country in any field. Write about that man or woman and why you think this person deserved the award.

5. Write a short biography of one of the Nobel prize winners who interests you.

## H. Crossword Puzzle: Alfred Nobel

### Across Clues

1. You and I
2. I met John yesterday. _____ mother is visiting him.
4. Alfred Nobel's _____ was Swedish.
5. I don't want people to forget me. I want them to _____ me.
7. Laura and I like _____ class.
9. _____ is the explosive that made Nobel rich.
11. Bombs, guns, and tanks are powerful _____ .
12. Bombs are _____ . They blow up when they hit something.

### Down Clues

1. A _____ states how a person wishes his or her possessions to be distributed after death.
2. A _____ is the title of a newspaper story.
3. Alfred Nobel wanted to _____ , or create, a device that was safe to use.
6. I have _____ pen. Do you have your pen?
8. Disturbed
9. Unsafe
10. Chemistry is a _____ of study.
13. The opposite of **war**
14. Certain
15. Build

16. The Nobel prize is an
    _____ for a person's
    achievements.
17. Nobel hated fighting and war. He
    hated all kinds of _____ .
19. Nine million dollars is a lot of
    money. To some people it is a
    _____ .

21. Error

18. I, you, _____ , she, it
20. I called Sam on the phone. I spoke
    to _____ for a short time.

---

## I. CLOZE Quiz

be          know          think
become      make          write
have        read

Read the passage below. Fill in each space with the simple past tense of one
of the verbs listed above. You may use the words more than once.

After Nobel (1) ___read___ the newspaper story, he *was*
(2) ___or became___ very upset about the image that the world
(3) ___had___ of him. He (4) ___thought___ about his problem
for years. Then, in 1895, an adventurer named Salomon August Andrée
(5) ___made___ plans to reach the North Pole. People all over the world *were*
(6) ___or became___ excited about Andrée's journey. Nobel (7) ___read___
about Andrée's plan, too, and (8) ___had___ an inspiration. He finally
(9) ___knew___ what to do with his fortune, and he (10) ___wrote___
his Last Will and Testament to give instructions for his plan.

Alfred Nobel died on December 10, 1896. He (11) ___was___ unmarried, and (12) ___had___ no children. People all over the world
(13) ___were___ amazed when they (14) ___read___ in the newspapers about Alfred Nobel's plan. However, after his death, the Nobel prize
(15) ___became___ the greatest honor that a person could achieve.

# CHAPTER 12

## Marie Curie: A 20th-Century Woman

Text

## Prereading Preparation

1. Look at the photograph on the left. Who is this a picture of? What kind of work did she do? Why was she an unusual woman?
2. Gold, oxygen, copper, and carbon are a few of the 103 elements. What are some other elements?
3. What are X rays? How are they dangerous? How are they useful?
4. What does it mean to be a 20th-century man or woman?

1   Marya Sklodowska was born on November 7, 1867, in
2   Poland. Marya's father wanted his five children to become well
3   educated. Unfortunately, the family was poor. In fact, Marya
4   supported her older sister Bronya for six years, until she fin-
5   ished medical school at the Sorbonne in Paris. Then, in 1891,
6   23-year-old Marya Sklodowska went to Paris to begin her own
7   education.
8       Once she arrived in Paris, Marya changed her name to the
9   French form, Marie. After living with Bronya and her husband
10  for a short time, she moved to an inexpensive apartment near
11  the university so she could study without interruption. Marie's
12  student life was extremely poor, but in spite of her difficult liv-
13  ing conditions, she was happy.
14      In July 1893, Marie passed her physics examination first in
15  her class. At this time she met Pierre Curie, a young scientist.
16  Marie and Pierre discovered that they had much in common.
17  They both believed that science was the most important part of

18  their lives. They didn't care about money or about being com-
19  fortable. They fell in love and were married on July 26, 1895.
20      Marie and Pierre Curie were very happy. They discussed
21  their work and the latest scientific events, such as the discov-
22  ery of X rays.* Marie was interested in this research and
23  began to look for unknown elements that had such rays.
24  Pierre Curie stopped his own research in order to help Marie
25  in her work. He realized that she was about to make an
26  important discovery.
27      In 1898, the Curies found two new elements that give off
28  radiation. They named these elements polonium and radium.
29  In those days, no one knew that such radioactive materials
30  were dangerous. In fact, Marie Curie created the word
31  **radioactive** to describe these materials. They did not know
32  that exposure to this radioactivity caused their constant
33  fatigue and illnesses, and they kept working. Finally, in 1902,
34  they proved the existence of radium.
35      On June 25, 1903, Marie became the first woman to
36  receive a doctor of science degree from the Sorbonne. Then
37  she received an even greater award. In 1903, the Academy of
38  Science at Stockholm, Sweden, awarded the Nobel prize in
39  physics to Marie and Pierre Curie and Henri Becquerel for
40  their discoveries in radioactivity.
41      The Curies continued to work closely together until a tragic
42  event occurred. On a rainy day in April 1906, Pierre was killed
43  in a street accident. Marie was heartbroken, but she continued
44  working. Then, in 1910, she isolated radium. It was the biggest
45  accomplishment of Marie Curie's career. In 1911, she received
46  the Nobel prize again, in chemistry. She was the first woman to
47  receive the Nobel prize and the first person to receive it a sec-
48  ond time.
49      Over the years, Marie's constant exposure to radiation con-
50  tinued to destroy her health. She died on July 4, 1934, from an
51  illness caused by her life's work: radium.
52      Marie Curie never cared about making any money from her
53  discoveries. Her life had been one of hard work, perseverance,
54  and self-sacrifice. However, in her personal life she was happily
55  married and had two daughters. Professionally, she made
56  important discoveries and achieved greatness in her field.

---

*X rays: An invisible, high-energy form of light that can pass through many
solid objects, such as the human body.

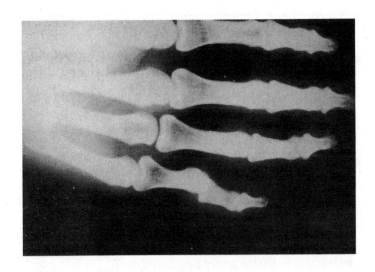

## A. Fact-Finding Exercise

Read the passage once. Then read the following statements. Check whether they are true (T) or false (F). If a statement is false, change the statement so that it is true. Then go back to the passage and find the line that supports your answer.

___✓ T ___F 1. Marya Sklodowska was Marie Curie.

_____

___ T ___F 2. Marie Curie was born in Paris.

*she was born in Poland*

___ T ___F 3. Marie went to the university in Poland.

*she went to the university in Paris*

___ T ___F 4. Marie's husband, Pierre, was a scientist.

_____

___✓ T ___F 5. The Curies discovered two new elements.

_____

___✓ T ___F 6. Radium made the Curies feel tired and sick.

_____

___✓ T ___F 7. Marie Curie was the first person to receive the Nobel prize.

*she was the first woman to receive the Nobel prize*

___✓ T ___F 8. Marie Curie won the Nobel prize twice.

_____

___ T ___F 9. Marie Curie wanted to earn a lot of money.

*she did not want to earn a lot of money*

## B. Information Recall

Read the passage a second time. Then try to answer the following questions. Do not look back at the passage. Compare your answers with a classmate's answers.

1. a. How old was Marie Curie when she went to study in Paris?

   _____

   b. Why did she start her education so late?

   _____

   _____

2. a. Where did Marie Curie meet her husband?

   _____

   b. How were Marie and Pierre similar?

   _____

   _____

3. What scientific research did the Curies do?

   _____

   _____

4. a. What elements did the Curies discover?

   _____

   b. What did they receive as a result of their discovery?

   _____

5. a. What was the biggest accomplishment of Marie Curie's life?

   _____

   b. What were some of Marie Curie's other great achievements?

   _____

   _____

6. a. When did Marie Curie die?

   _____

   b. What caused her death?

   _____

## C. Reading Analysis

Read each question carefully. Either circle the letter of the correct answer, or write your answer in the space provided.

1.  What is the main idea of this passage?
    a.   Marie Curie discovered two new elements, polonium and radium.
    b. ╱ Marie Curie was a great scientist who won the Nobel prize two times.
    c.   Marie Curie did research on radioactive materials for many years.

2.  Marya's father wanted his five children to become well educated. **Unfortunately**, the family was poor.
    a.   How many brothers and sisters did Marya have?
        1. ╱ four
        2.   five
        3.   six
    b.   This sentence means that
        1.   none of the children went to school
        2.   all the children went to school
        3. ╱ the family could not afford to send the children to school
    c.   Complete the following sentence correctly.

        Marie and Pierre Curie worked well together for many years. Unfortunately,
        1. ╱ Pierre died when he was still young
        2.   Pierre and Marie discovered two new elements
        3.   Pierre and Marie shared the Nobel prize in 1903

3.  The family was poor. **In fact**, Marya **supported** her older sister Bronya until she finished medical school at the **Sorbonne** in Paris.
    a.   This sentence means that
        1.   Marya lived with her sister
        2. ╱ Marya gave her sister money to live on
        3.   Marya helped her sister study
    b.   What information follows **in fact**?
        1. ╱ additional information that gives more details about the previous sentence
        2.   different information that introduces a new idea
    c.   The **Sorbonne** is
        1.   a business
        2.   a hospital
        3. ╱ a school

4. **Once** she arrived in Paris, Marya changed her name to the French form, Marie.

   In this sentence, **once** means
   a. one time
   b. when
   c. before

5. Marya's student life was very poor, but **in spite of** her difficult **living conditions**, she was happy.
   a. This sentence means that
      1. Marya's living conditions made her happy because they were difficult
      2. Marya's living conditions were bad, but she was happy
   b. Read the following sentences. Write **in spite of** in the correct space.
      1. John was very sick. _In spite of_ his illness, he went to work.
      2. John was very sick. _Because of_ his illness, he went to the hospital.
   c. **Living conditions** refers to the fact that
      1. Marya lived in a cold, uncomfortable apartment and ate little food
      2. Marya was a student and had to study hard

6. In July 1893, Marie passed her physics exam **first in her class**. **At this time** she met Pierre Curie, a young scientist.
   a. What does **first in her class** mean?
      1. Marie graduated before all the other students.
      2. Marie was the best student in her class.
   b. **At this time** means
      1. at the same time she passed her exam
      2. in the 1890s
      3. during this time period

7. Marie and Pierre Curie discussed their work and the latest scientific events, such as the discovery of **X rays**.
   a. What are **X rays**?

      _____

   b. How do you know?

      _____

   c. This kind of information is called a

      _____

8. Pierre Curie stopped his own research **in order to** help Marie.
   a. Pierre Curie stopped his own research
      1. ╱ because he wanted to help Marie
      2. because he wanted to tell Marie what to do
   b. What follows **in order to**?
      1. an example
      2. a result
      3. ╱ a reason

9. Pierre realized that Marie was **about to** make an important discovery.

   **About to** means
   a. ╱ the time immediately before something happens
   b. the time immediately after something happens
   c. at the moment something is happening

10. In 1898, the Curies found two new elements that give off radiation. They named these elements polonium and radium. In those days, no one knew that such radioactive materials were dangerous.

    What does **such radioactive materials** refer to?

    ___Polonium and radium_____

11. Marie Curie created the term **radioactive** to describe these materials.

    This sentence means that
    a. ╱ Marie Curie was the first person to use the word **radioactive**
    b. Marie Curie invented these radioactive materials

12. The Curies continued to work closely together **until** a **tragic** event occurred. On a rainy day in April 1906, Pierre was killed in a street accident. Marie was **heartbroken**, but she continued working.
    a. **Until** means
       1. ╱ up to the time when something happens
       2. up to the time when something stops working
    b. Read the following sentences. Write the word **until** in the correct space.
       1. John studied very hard __before__ he finished the exam.
       2. ╱ John studied very hard __until__ the exam began.
    c. The word **tragic** means
       1. very violent
       2. ╱ very sad
       3. very surprising

   d.   **Heartbroken** means that
      1.   Marie was very unhappy
      2.   Marie became very sick

13. **Over the years**, Marie's constant exposure to radiation continued to destroy her health.

   **Over the years** means
   a.   in the years immediately before Marie died
   b.   through all the years that she worked

14. Marie Curie's life had been one of hard work, **perseverance**, and self-sacrifice. However, in her personal life she was happy, and professionally she achieved greatness in her **field**.
   a.   Think about Marie Curie's life. What does the characteristic of **perseverance** mean?
      1.   Marie Curie had a sad life.
      2.   Marie Curie never stopped trying.
      3.   Marie Curie had little money.
   b.   What was Marie Curie's **field**?
      1.   Paris
      2.   career
      3.   science

## D. Word Forms

### Part 1

In English, verbs change to nouns in several ways. Some verbs become nouns by adding the suffixes *-ance* or *-ence*, for example, *persist* (v.), *persistence* (n.).

Complete each sentence with the correct form of the words on the left. Be careful of spelling changes. **Write all the verbs in the simple past tense. They may be affirmative or negative. The nouns may be singular or plural.**

occur (v.) *biến cố*
occurrence (n.)

1. There were several _____ *s* of Janet's illness before she began to get well. Then her illness _____ *ed* again, and she was very unhappy.

exist (v.) *tồn tại*
existence (n.) *hiện hữu*

2. For one hundred years, no one could prove the _____ of the ninth planet. Then, in 1930, Clyde Tombaugh proved that Pluto _____ *ed* when he located it through a telescope.

persevere (v.) *kiên trì, dốc sức*
perseverance (n.) *trì bỉ*

3. Henry was having a lot of trouble learning calculus, but he __*did not*__. Because he had no _____, he gave up, and failed his exams.

assist (v.) *giúp đỡ*
assistance (n.)

4. When Andrew registered for classes, he needed some _____ . Unfortunately, no one _____ *ed* him, and he filled out all the forms incorrectly.

assure (v.) *bảo liễm, bảo đảm*
assurance (n.)

5. Edward, my brother, __*did not*__ me enough that plane travel was safe: in spite of all his _____ *s*, I was very frightened on my first plane trip.

## Part 2

In English, some adjectives become nouns by adding the suffix -*ness*, for example *sick* (adj.), *sickness* (n.)

Complete each sentence with the correct form of the words on the left. **The nouns may be singular or plural.**

ill (adj.)
illness (n.)

1. It seems that Beverly is always _____.
   In fact, she has had four different _____*es*
   so far this year.

great (adj.)
greatness (n.)

2. Natalie has a reputation as a _____ tennis
   player. She has won many international competi-
   tions, and news of her _____*ss* is spreading
   around the world.

happy (adj.)
happiness (n.)

3. Alex and Victoria's _____*ss* is not accidental.
   They get along well, they have jobs they like, and
   they live in a comfortable home. Naturally, they
   are very _____ with their lives.

short (adj.)
shortness (n.)

4. It is a very _____ distance between Larry's
   house and the health club. The _____*ss* of
   the trip makes it easy for Larry to exercise there
   every day.

near (adj.)
nearness (n.)

5. The shopping center is quite _____
   Shirley's house. Because of the center's _____*ss*
   to her home, she walks there almost every day.

## E. Vocabulary in Context

| | | |
|---|---|---|
| about to | finally (adv.) 9 | interruptions (n.) 6 |
| achieved (v.) 5 | in order to 4 | supported (v.) 7 |
| discovery (n.) 8 | in spite of 3 | unfortunately (adv.) 1 |
| exposure (n.) 2 | | |

Read each sentence below. Fill in each space with the correct word from the list above. Use each word only once.

1. Allen wanted to see his friend Michael yesterday. _____, Michael had to stay home to study for an English test.

2. Doctors believe that _____ to the sun for many years can cause skin cancer.

3. _____ the beautiful sunny weather, Donna stayed in the house all day.

4. _____ grow healthy plants, keep them in the sun and give them water frequently.

5. Ann worked for many years before she _____ success in her field.

6. I have to study for my math exam. I don't want any _____. Please do not talk to me or play loud music.

7. Catherine's parents _____ her when she lost her job. Fortunately, she found another job in three months.

8. The _____ of America changed people's ideas about the world forever.

9. We looked for our cat for several hours. We _____ found it. It was hiding behind the garage.

10. Louise looked up at the sky. It was _____ rain, and she did not have an umbrella, so she ran home to avoid getting wet.

## F. Follow-up Activities

1. Go to the library and find out more information about Marie and Pierre's two daughters, Irene and Eve. For example, when were they born? What did they do? Were they scientists, too? Did they become well-known, too? Compare your information with your classmates' information.
2. A biography is the story of a person's life. Prepare a biography of an important person from your country. Give an oral presentation about this person to your class.
3. Work in pairs or small groups. Make a list of the five most important discoveries of the 20th century. Remember, a discovery is something a person *finds*, something that exists. An invention is something a person *creates*, such as the telephone, the light bulb, the automobile. Combine your list with the other groups' lists. Together, choose the three most important discoveries.

## G. Topics for Discussion and Writing

1. a.   What is a 20th-century woman? How can you describe a 20th-century woman?
   b.   How does Marie Curie fit your description of a 20th-century woman?
2. Marie Curie supported her sister Bronya when Bronya was in medical school. Then, when Bronya finished school, Marie began her own education. Why do you think Marie did this? What kind of person do you think she was? Would you support your sister or brother if you could? Explain your reasons.
3. Marie Curie made a lot of sacrifices for her work. She never made any money from her discoveries, and she died from her life's work: radium. Do you know of any other individuals who sacrificed their lives for their work? Do you think you could sacrifice your life for your work? Why, or why not? Explain your reasons.
4. Work was the most important part of Marie Curie's life. What is the most important part of your life? What do you think the most important part of your life will be in the future? Explain your answer.
5. Write your autobiography or the biography of someone you know personally and whom you admire.

# H. Crossword Puzzle: Marie Curie

## Across Clues

6. A death is a very _____ occurrence.
8. Unhappily; unluckily.
11. Give someone money to help him or her live or go to school
12. I
13. When you find something for the first time, you make a _____ .
14. Past participle of **put**
17. Sickness
18. Past participle of **hit**
20. Polonium, radium, gold, and iron are all _____ .
22. The opposite of **yes**
23. _____ to X rays or to the sun's rays can cause injury to the body.
26. After a long time

## Down Clues

1. Achievement
2. Something that causes a break in your work is an _____ .
3. Past participle of **go**
4. Past participle of **run**
5. If you do not give up easily, you have _____ .
7. The Nobel prize is an important _____ .
9. Polonium, radium, uranium, and plutonium are all _____ elements.
10. Past participle of **lost**
15. Past participle of **lend**
16. Harmful
19. _____ , two, three
21. Past participle of **show**
24. The opposite of **down**
25. Every

## I. CLOZE Quiz

| he | she | they |
|----|-----|------|
| his | her | their |

Read the passage below. Fill in each space with one of the pronouns listed above. You may use the words more than once.

In 1891, 23-year-old Marya Sklodowska went to Paris to begin

(1) _____ education. Once (2) _____ arrived in Paris, Marya

changed (3) _____ name to the French form, Marie. After living

with Bronya and (4) _____ husband for a short time,

(5) _____ moved near the university so (6) _____ could

study without interruption. Marie's student life was extremely poor, but in

spite of (7) _____ difficult living conditions, (8) _____ was

happy.

In July 1893, Marie passed (9) _____ physics examination first

in (10) _____ class. At this time (11) _____ met Pierre

Curie. (12) _____ was a young scientist. Marie and Pierre discovered

that (13) _____ had much in common. (14) _____ both

believed that science was the most important part of (15) _____

lives. (16) _____ fell in love and were married on July 26, 1895.

Marie and Pierre Curie were very happy. (17) _____ discussed

(18) _____ work and the latest scientific events. Marie began to do

research on X rays. Pierre Curie stopped (19) _____ own research in

order to help Marie in (20) _____ work. (21) _____ realized

that (22) _____ was about to make an important discovery.

## Unit VI Discussion

1. Marie Curie won two Nobel prizes for her achievements in science. Do you think Marie Curie's work agrees with Alfred Nobel's idea of special achievement? Explain your answer.
2. Would you like to win a Nobel prize? How? In what category? Nobel prize winners receive approximately $225,000 in prize money. What would you do with the money?

# Index to Key Words and Phrases

# Answer Key

## Chapter 1. Elephants: Gentle Giants of the Earth

### Exercise A

1. T
2. F.  Male elephants weigh about six tons. OR Female elephants weigh about three tons.
3. F.  Elephants eat only plants.
4. F.  The number of elephants in Africa is decreasing.
5. T

### Exercise B

1. Elephants live with their relatives. They show emotions such as joy, sorrow, anger, patience, and friendliness. They become excited when they meet old friends.
2. (a) It can weigh six tons and be 12 feet tall.
   (b) It weighs about three tons and is about eight feet tall.
   (c) It weighs about 260 pounds (260 lb) and is about three feet tall.
3. Its trunk. An elephant uses it to smell, wash, eat, drink, "talk," and hug.
4. Some people kill elephants to make money by selling their tusks.

### Exercise C

1. a
2. (a) 3
   (b) 1
3. about three tons
4. (a) 2
   (b) 2
   (c) 1
5. (a) yes
   (b) no

6. (a) 2
   (b) 1
7. (a) unusual
   (b) 1
   (c) characteristic
   (d) 2
8. c
9. a
10. (a) 1
    (b) as a result
    (c) 2
    (d) 2
    (e) 1
    (f) 3
11. a

## Exercise D

### Part 1
1. protect / protection
2. attracts / attractions
3. cooperation / cooperate
4. fascination / fascinate
5. continue / continuation

### Part 2
1. uses n. / don't use v.
2. doesn't practice v. / practice n.
3. walks n. / doesn't walk v.
4. doesn't decrease v. / decrease n.
5. value n. / don't value v.

## Exercise E

1. protect
2. extinct
3. features
4. heads
5. cooperation
6. unusual
7. fascinating
8. unfortunately
9. as a result
10. ability

## Exercise F

1. Answers will vary.
2. Answers will vary.
3. Answers will vary.

4. (a) three tons
   (b) 1
   (c) 260 pounds (260 lb)
   (d) 3
   (e) 12 feet
   (f) 2
   (g) three feet
   (h) 2
5. (a) Central African Republic
   (b) Kenya
   (c) Central African Republic
   (d) 2

## Exercise G

Answers will vary.

## Exercise H

**Across Clues**
1. Africa
7. emotions
8. feature
11. elephant
13. ornaments
14. out
15. fascinating
18. ivory
19. money
20. no
21. top
22. tusks
24. yes

**Down Clues**
2. cooperate
3. but
4. not
5. off
6. trunk
7. extinct
9. consequently
10. vegetarian
12. practice
15. forget
16. ten
17. giants
23. up

## Exercise I

1. are
2. weighs
3. is, stands
4. weigh
5. are, stand
6. weighs
7. is, stands
8. have
9. grow
10. lives
11. reach

12. use
13. do not use
14. do not eat
15. eat

---

## Chapter 2. The Extinction of the Dinosaurs

### Exercise A

1. T
2. T
3. F.  Some dinosaurs ate meat.
4. T
5. F.  The dirt decreased the Earth's temperature.
6. F.  They do not know exactly where the comet struck.

### Exercise B

1. (a)  because they want to learn about dinosaurs.
   (b)  You can see skeletons, footprints in stone, and ancient eggs.
2. (a)  three theories
   (b)  because the plants died.
   (c)  No; none of the theories explained all the extinctions.
3. (a)  in the 1980s
   (b)  They think it struck the Earth near Mexico.
   (c)  It was 25 miles deep and 100 miles in diameter.
   (d)  It decreased.
   (e)  because the temperature became colder and there was not enough sunlight.
4.  They need to find the place where the comet or asteroid struck the Earth.

### Exercise C

1. c
2. (a)  giant
   (b)  3
   (c)  animals
3. (a)  2
   (b)  1
4. (a)  1
   (b)  3
   (c)  2
   (d)  slowly
5. a
6. (a)  2
   (b)  2

7. (a) 3
   (b) 2
   (c) 2
8. (a) 2
   (b) quickly
   (c) 1
9. (a) 3
   (b) 1
   (c) place
   (d) 3

## Exercise D

**Part 1**
1. exact / exactly
2. incredibly / incredible
3. significant / significantly
4. rapid / rapidly
5. gradual / gradually

**Part 2**
1. changes n. / changed v.
2. visited v. / visits n.
3. damage n. / damaged v.
4. cover n. / didn't cover v.
5. decreased v. / decrease n.

## Exercise E

1. uncertain
2. giant
3. prove
4. creature
5. climate
6. theory
7. in fact
8. discuss
9. incredibly
10. simply

## Exercise F

Answers will vary.

## Exercise G

Answers will vary.

## Exercise H

| **Across Clues** | **Down Clues** |
|---|---|
| 2. am | 1. sunlight |
| 6. dinosaurs | 2. asteroid |
| 7. no | 3. giant |
| 8. me | 4. is |
| 10. did | 5. gradually |
| 12. creatures | 8. museum |
| 13. extinct | 9. per |
| 14. climate | 11. diameter |
| 16. theory | 15. vegetarian |
| 20. prove | 17. ate |
| 21. decrease | 18. Mexico |
| 22. significantly | 19. up |
| 24. location | 23. yes |
| 25. ton | |

## Exercise I

1. began
2. struck
3. struck
4. was
5. created
6. blew
7. covered
8. blocked
9. decreased
10. died
11. was
12. died
13. had
14. was

---

# Chapter 3. The All-American Diner

## Exercise A

1. T
2. F.  They began as simple food carts.
3. T
4. F.  He built the first diner big enough for people to come inside.
5. F.  The original menu became bigger.
6. T

**Exercise B**

1. (a) They began as simple food carts.
   (b) Late-night workers ate there.
2. The menus became bigger. They included more foods. They included all three meals.
3. From the outside, they are usually rectangular buildings with large windows. On the inside, they have counters with stools, booths, and tables and chairs.
4. They became big, permanent buildings. They allow people to come inside and sit down. They serve all three meals. They are often open around the clock.
5. 4, 3, 1, 2, 5

**Exercise C**

1. a
2. b
3. (a) 1
   (b) 4
   (c) 2
4. (a) 2
   (b) 2
5. (a) 1
   (b) 1
   (c) The original menu became bigger, and diners became permanent buildings.
   (d) 3
   (e) 2
6. (a) 2
   (b) They are fast-food restaurants.
   (c) 2
7. (a) at a table with chairs
   (b) at the counter on a stool
   (c) in a booth

**Exercise D**

1. quickly / quick
2. original / originally
3. permanent / permanently
4. simple / simply
5. usual / usually

## Exercise E

1. in addition
2. popular
3. include
4. customer
5. service
6. enough
7. allow
8. however

## Exercise F

Answers will vary.

## Exercise G

Answers will vary.

## Exercise H

**Across Clues**

1. however
4. were
6. coffee
8. yes
11. not
12. meals
14. big
15. wheels
16. permanent
19. breakfast
20. every
21. counter
22. no
24. customer
26. up

**Down Clues**

1. hi
2. workers
3. very
5. rectangular
7. fast
9. am
10. favorite
13. restaurant
17. never
18. carts
21. clock
23. menu
25. top

## Exercise I

1. the
2. the
3. a
4. the
5. an
6. the
7. the
8. the

9. a
10. a
11. the
12. a
13. an
14. the
15. the

---

## Chapter 4. The Birth of the United States

### Exercise A

1. F.  It is the fourth largest country in the world.
2. T
3. T
4. F.  He wrote it with other people in a committee.
5. T
6. F.  George Washington became the first president in 1789.

### Exercise B

1. They decided to become independent because the king did not listen to the colonist's complaints.
2. The purpose of the Continental Congress was to give the colonists representation, and to discuss problems.
3. It was so difficult because the Americans had few arms and clothes, and very little money, and because it was so long.
4. He was the commander-in-chief of the army during the American Revolution, and he was the first president of the United States.

### Exercise C

1. b
2. (a) 1
   (b) nation
   (c) 2
   (d) 2
3. (a) British
   (b) 1
4. (a) illegal
   (b) because the first meeting was in secret
5. (a) 1
   (b) 1 and 3
6. b
7. (a) 2
   (b) 2

8. a
9. (a) 1
   (b) 2
10. (a) Joyce and her mother
    (b) 2

## Exercise D

**Part 1**
1. collected / collection
2. discussion / discussed
3. created / creation
4. decision / decided
5. organization / organized
6. declared / declaration

**Part 2**
1. practiced v. / practice n.
2. compromised v. / compromise n.
3. trust n. / trusted v.
4. respected v. / respect n.

## Exercise E

1. committee
2. unavoidable
3. few
4. refused
5. complaint
6. authority
7. unanimously
8. obeyed
9. arms
10. honest

## Exercise F

1. (2) June 1776. The Continental Congress organized the colonies into states.
   (3) July 4, 1776. The beginning of the American Revolution.
   (4) September 3, 1783. The British signed a peace treaty. A new nation was born.
   (5) December 7, 1787. The states began to accept the new Constitution and the new central government.
   (6) April 30, 1789. George Washington became president of the United States.
2. Answers will vary.
3. Answers will vary.

## Exercise G

Answers will vary.

## Exercise H

### Across Clues

4. experienced
7. elect
10. had
11. unanimously
14. understood
15. committee
16. arms
17. on
18. country
19. chiefly
20. saw
21. trust
22. lay
23. basis
25. British

### Down Clues

1. fell
2. read
3. were
5. declaration
6. ran
8. showed
9. put
12. compromise
13. democracy
14. unavoidable
16. authority
18. colonies
22. lost
24. or

## Exercise I

1. to
2. of
3. in
4. on
5. to
6. for
7. at
8. of
9. to
10. to
11. to
12. in
13. of
14. to
15. of
16. for
17. of
18. of
19. on
20. on

## Chapter 5. Twins: How Alike Are They?

### Exercise A

1. T
2. F.  They never lived together.
3. F.  Identical twins who did not grow up together help scientists understand them better.
4. F.  They were not separated at birth, and they grew up together.
5. T
6. T

### Exercise B

1. Both men were married twice. Their first wives were both named Linda, and their second wives were both named Betty. Both twins named their first sons James Allan, drove blue Chevrolets, and had dogs named Toy.
2. (a)  They studied 350 sets of identical twins who did not grow up together.
   (b)  They wanted to understand the connection between environment and biology.
   (c)  They learned that personality characteristics are really inherited.
3. John Fuller tells people he is Buell, and Buell Fuller tells people he is John. They like to confuse people.
4. Donald concentrated very hard, and Louis telephoned him.

### Exercise C

1. c
2. (a)  3
   (b)  2
   (c)  1
3. a
4. b
5. b
6. (a)  Jim Springer and Jim Lewis
   (b)  1
7. (a)  Jenny met her sister in the restaurant.
   (b)  2
8. (a)  sets
   (b)  environment
   (c)  4
9. (a)  friendliness, shyness, fears
   (b)  such as
   (c)  2

10. (a)  Extrasensory Perception: the ability to feel something that people cannot feel with the five senses.
    (b)  There is a star after ESP that tells the reader to look at the bottom of the page for an explanation.
    (c)  2
11. (a)  Donald Keith and Louis Keith
    (b)  2
12. sure

## Exercise D

### Part 1

1. close / closeness
2. sure / sureness
3. openness / open
4. friendly / friendliness
5. shyness / shy

### Part 2

1. influence n. / influence v.
2. fears n. / fears v.
3. experiences v. / experience n.
4. doesn't work v. / work n.
5. telephone n. / telephones v.

## Exercise E

1. similar
2. influences
3. close
4. pair
5. concentrates
6. identical
7. environment
8. personality
9. inherited
10. coincidence

## Exercise F

Answers will vary.

## Exercise G

Answers will vary.

## Exercise H

**Across Clues**

1. before
5. coincidence
9. both
11. curious
12. among
13. on
14. down
16. at
17. inherited
19. identical
21. uncertain
23. researcher
24. below
26. under
27. behind

**Down Clues**

2. over
3. with
4. personality
5. close
6. concentrate
7. environment
8. separate
10. against
15. between
18. influence
20. similar
22. from
25. out
27. by

## Exercise I

1. they
2. them
3. they
4. they
5. they
6. his
7. him
8. he
9. them
10. their
11. their
12. their
13. they
14. them

# Chapter 6. Adoption: The Search for Happiness

## Exercise A

1. T
2. F.   Some people adopt babies of different races.
3. F.   Most adopted children know they are adopted.
4. F.   It is difficult for adopted children to find their birth parents.
5. T
6. F.   He does not want to look for her.
7. T

## Exercise B

1. No; people adopt children of different ages, races, and sexes.
2. No; birth records of most adopted children are usually sealed.
3. No; he is afraid she would be awful, and he would be disappointed.
4. Sometimes she wants to look for her, but sometimes she doesn't.
5. Yes; they need to know where they came from, and they need to know what their medical history is.

## Exercise C

1. a
2. (a) 1
   (b) 2
   (c) 2
   (d) 3
3. babies
4. (a) 1
   (b) white, black, Asian
   (c) 2
   (d) 3
   (e) 2
5. a
6. (a) 1
   (b) , or
   (c) 7
   (d) 1
   (e) documents
   (f) 2
   (g) 3
7. (a) 1
   (b) 2
   (c) 1

8. (a) 3
   (b) 1
   (c) 2
9. (a) 3
   (b) 1
   (c) 2
10. (a) 2
    (b) 1
    (c) 1

## Exercise D

**Part 1**

1. decides / decisions
2. does not inform / information
3. does not react / reactions
4. does not protect / protection
5. adopts / adoption

**Part 2**

1. plans n. / plans v.
2. care n. / care v.
3. records n. / does not record v.
4. search v. / search n.
5. worries n. / does not worry v.

## Exercise E

1. naturally
2. worthwhile
3. beforehand
4. as a matter of fact
5. searches
6. confidential
7. in any case
8. mixed feelings
9. includes
10. sealed

## Exercise F

Answers will vary.

## Exercise G

Answers will vary.

## Exercise H

### Across Clues
1. its
5. adopt
7. reaction
8. naturally
12. beforehand
15. race
16. now
18. adoptees
19. sealed
21. couple
22. their
23. very

### Down Clues
1. infants
2. decide
3. his
4. confidential
6. our
9. yes
10. worthwhile
11. search
13. birth parents
14. documents
17. her
20. your
21. care

## Exercise I

1. their
2. them
3. they
4. I
5. I
6. my
7. I
8. I
9. I
10. she
11. her
12. my
13. I
14. she
15. she
16. her
17. she
18. I
19. I
20. I
21. her
22. my
23. she
24. me
25. I

## Chapter 7. Secondhand Smoke

### Exercise A

1. T
2. F.   Her husband, Edward Gilson, has lung cancer.
3. T
4. F.   Many people die from secondhand smoke.
5. T
6. F.   You cannot smoke on short domestic airline flights.

### Exercise B

1. He breathed in secondhand smoke for 35 years.
2. (a) It is the smoke from one person's cigarette that another person breathes in.
   (b) because all cigarette smoke is harmful
3. (a) because they live with their smoking parents. As a result, they have no choice.
   (b) They are sick more often than children who live in homes where no one smokes. These effects continue when they are adults, too.
4. Some laws prohibit smoking in public places and on short domestic airline flights.

### Exercise C

1. b
2. a
3. (a) 1
   (b) 2
4. (a) secondhand smoke
   (b) 1
   (c) 3
   (d) It is a government department that is responsible for protecting the U.S. environment, particularly the air and water.
   (e) There is a star after **Environmental Protection Agency** that tells the reader to look at the bottom of the page for an explanation.
   (f) 2
5. a
6. (a) toxic
   (b) 2
7. (a) 3
   (b) 1
8. a
9. a
10. a

11. (a) 3
    (b) forbid
    (c) 2
    (d) limit
    (e) , or
    (f) 1
    (g) a flight within a country

## Exercise D

### Part 1

1. reports n. / reports v.
2. damages v. / damage n.
3. do not limit v. / limit n.
4. studies n. / studies v.
5. does not result v. / results n.

### Part 2

1. sick / sickness
2. aware / awareness
3. near / nearness
4. late / latenesses
5. weakness / weak

## Exercise E

1. exposure
2. realizes
3. toxic
4. as a matter of fact
5. nevertheless
6. prohibits
7. recently
8. disease
9. harmful
10. avoids

## Exercise F

Answers will vary.

## Exercise G

Answers will vary.

## Exercise H

| Across Clues | Down Clues |
|---|---|
| 1. avoid | 1. am |
| 4. twice | 2. domestic |
| 5. pack | 3. risk |
| 6. top | 7. cancer |
| 9. secondhand | 8. harmful |
| 12. prohibit | 10. even |
| 14. i.e. | 11. nonsmoker |
| 15. poisonous | 13. bronchitis |
| 17. push | 16. healthy |
| 18. tobacco | 19. quit |
| 21. public | 20. lungs |
| 22. currently | |
| 23. go | |

## Exercise I

1. to
2. of
3. in
4. of
5. for
6. for
7. in
8. in
9. of
10. of
11. in
12. of
13. to

# Chapter 8. A Healthy Diet for Everyone

## Exercise A

1. T
2. F.  The amount of each food group to eat is changing.
3. T
4. F.  Most Japanese eat a lot of grains. OR Most Japanese eat very little meat.
5. F.  There are very low rates of cancer and heart disease in Japan.
6. T
7. F.  It is very important for children to have a healthy diet.

8. F.  Children usually eat the same way their parents eat.
9. F.  Doctors believe that fruit and vegetables prevent different diseases.

## Exercise B

1. (a) yes
   (b) because they eat a lot of meat and only a small amount of grains, fruit, and vegetables
2. (a) no
   (b) because they eat a lot of grains and very little meat
3. (a) Their rates of cancer and heart disease increase.
   (b) because their diet changes
4. (a) The disease rates in these countries are increasing.
   (b) because the diets of people in these countries are changing
5. (a) Eating fruit and vegetables can prevent some diseases.
   (b) Eating meat can cause some diseases.

## Exercise C

1. a
2. (a) 2
   (b) 3
3. type
4. (a) It is a department that is responsible for controlling the quality of food in the United States.
   (b) There is a star after **USDA** that tells the reader to look at the bottom of the page for an explanation.
   (c) footnote
   (d) 1. meat: meat, fish, chicken
       2. dairy: milk, cheese, butter
       3. grains: bread, cereals, rice
       4. fruit and vegetables
   (e) 1
5. (a) 2
   (b) 1
   (c) 1
6. (a) 2
   (b) 1
   (c) 2
   (d) hamburgers and ice cream
   (e) 3
7. (a) 1
   (b) 3
   (c) 2
8. (a) 3
   (b) 1

9.  (a)  2
    (b)  1
10. (a)  2
    (b)  1
    (c)  3
    (d)  2

## Exercise D

**Part 1**

1.  improvements / improve
2.  does not agree / agreement
3.  encourages / encouragement
4.  develop / development
5.  do not enjoy / enjoyment

**Part 2**

1.  does not research v. / research n.
2.  increases v. / increase n.
3.  taste n. / do not taste v.
4.  causes n. / causes v.
5.  changes n. / does not change v.

## Exercise E

1.  confused
2.  unfortunately
3.  describe
4.  prevent
5.  as a result
6.  suggestion
7.  type
8.  agree
9.  disease
10. because of

## Exercise F

Answers will vary.

## Exercise G

Answers will vary.

## Exercise H

| Across Clues | Down Clues |
|---|---|
| 4. research | 1. is |
| 5. consequently | 2. daily |
| 7. no | 3. kind |
| 9. off | 5. cancer |
| 11. moreover | 6. unfortunately |
| 12. healthy | 8. or |
| 13. grains | 10. fruit |
| 14. prevent | 13. groups |
| 17. up | 15. dairy |
| 19. improvements | 16. confused |
| 20. yes | 18. are |
| 22. disease | 21. meat |
| 23. top | 22. diet |

## Exercise I

1. too much, a lot of, large amounts of
2. a lot of, too much, large amounts of
3. a small amount of
4. high rates of
5. a lot of, large amounts of
6. very little
7. very low rates of
8. more, a lot of
9. less
10. fewer

---

## Chapter 9. Oil: An Important World Resource  *Tài nguyên*

### Exercise A

1. T
2. F.   It began in 1859.
3. T
4. F.   It is not ready to use. People need to clean it.
5. T
6. F.   We use petroleum products every day.

### Exercise B

1. (a)  They used whale oil to light their lamps and to make candles.
   (b)  because many whales were killed, and it was very difficult to find them

2. (a) It becomes natural gas.
   (b) We use it to heat our homes and to cook with.
3. (a) It becomes asphalt.
   (b) We use it to pave roads and parking lots.
4. synthetic rubber and synthetic fibers, detergent, vitamins, drugs, plastic containers, toys, shampoo, lipstick, and hand lotion.

## Exercise C

1. c
2. b
3. (a) 3
   (b) 2
   (c) 3
4. b
5. (a) 2
   (b) 1
6. (a) 2
   (b) 3
7. c
8. (a) 2
   (b) synthetic fibers
   (c) such as
   (d) 1
   (e) They are natural fibers.
9. (a) 1
   (b) 3
   (c) 2

## Exercise D

**Part 1**
1. evaporation / evaporates
2. lubricates / lubrication
3. does not produce / production
4. prescriptions / do not prescribe
5. add / addition

**Part 2**
1. supply v. / supply n.
2. grease n. / greases v.
3. lights n. / does not light v.
4. do not heat v. / heat n.
5. processes n. / process v.

## Exercise E

1. refine
2. material
3. unfortunately
4. in fact
5. impure
6. complex
7. source

8. organic
9. mix
10. in other words

## Exercise F

1. (a) detergent
   (b) horses and wagons
   (c) whale oil and candles
   (d) wood and coal
   (e) asphalt
   (f) synthetic rubber
   (g) cotton, wool, and linen
2. (a) the Middle East
   (b) Europe
   (c) the former Soviet Union
   (d) 3

## Exercise G

Answers will vary.

## Exercise H

**Across Clues**

1. two
4. impure
6. in
7. hydrocarbons
13. asphalt
15. detergent
17. lightest
19. she
20. whales
22. no
23. petroleum
24. cars
25. sedimentary

**Down Clues**

2. wash
3. furnace
5. millions
8. on
9. aunt
10. barrels
11. up
12. synthetic
14. kerosene
16. grease
18. to
21. refine
23. past
26. top
27. yes

## Exercise I

1. was
2. was
3. is
4. is
5. is

6. are
7. are
8. were
9. were

---

# Chapter 10. Earthquakes: What Are They and How Do They Happen?

## Exercise A

1. F.  It is broken into many pieces.
2. T
3. F.  The plates move in several different directions.
4. T
5. F.  Scientists do not know when and where an earthquake will happen in the future. They cannot predict earthquakes.

## Exercise B

1. The crust of the Earth is the surface of the Earth. It is broken into a number of large pieces called plates, which are always moving.
2. (a) Earthquakes happen when plates move in different directions and cause the rocks to break.
   (b) Earthquakes can happen in four different ways.
   (c) First, they can happen when plates move apart. Second, they can happen when plates slide past one another. Third, they can happen when plates push directly against each other. Fourth, they can happen inside plates when they are squeezed.
3. (a) No, they can't.
   (b) People can design buildings, dams, and bridges that can resist earthquakes. They can teach the public how to prepare for and survive earthquakes.

## Exercise C

1. a
2. (a) 1
   (b) 2
3. surface
4. hot, melted rock
5. region, zone
6. (a) for instance
   (b) 3
7. (a) 2
   (b) 1

8. (a)  3
   (b)  2
9. (a)  1
   (b)  3
   (c)  2

## Exercise D

**Part 1**
1. move / movement
2. place / placement
3. announcements / do not announce
4. does not arrange / arrangements
5. requirement / require

**Part 2**
1. fear n. / fears v.
2. changes n. / do not change v.
3. ride v. / ride n.
4. cause v. / cause n.
5. designs n. / does not design v.

## Exercise E

1. predict
2. throughout
3. however
4. structures
5. apart
6. for example
7. resist
8. regions
9. furthermore
10. downward

## Exercise F

2. Answers will vary. They include the following: Take the mirror off the wall over the bed; remove heavy objects from the bookshelves next to the window; move the bed away from the window; move the chest of drawers further away from the bedroom door; take the lamp off the top of the chest of drawers; take the heavy picture off the wall next to the window.
3. (1)  yes
   (2)  no
   (3)  yes
   (4)  no
   (5)  yes
   (6)  yes
   (7)  yes
   (8)  no
   (9)  no
   (10)  yes

## Exercise G

Answers will vary.

## Exercise H

**Across Clues**

2. on
3. apart
5. push
8. predict
10. California
11. two
12. crust
14. however
15. directions
19. coast
20. earthquake
21. zone
22. slide
23. leave
24. slowly
25. scientists

**Down Clues**

1. broken
2. occur
4. resist
5. place
6. fear
7. continents
8. plates
9. too
13. downward
16. throughout
17. buildings
18. region
19. Central
24. she

## Exercise I

1. the
2. a
3. the
4. the
5. the
6. a
7. an
8. the
9. the
10. an
11. an
12. the
13. the
14. the
15. the
16. the
17. the
18. the
19. the
20. the

## Chapter 11. Alfred Nobel: A Man of Peace

### Exercise A

1. F.  He did not want people to remember him this way.
2. F.  He died in 1896. His brother died in 1888.
3. T
4. T
5. F.  Men and women can receive the Nobel prize.
6. F.  In 1895, Andrée planned an expedition to the North Pole.

### Exercise B

1. He became upset because the newspaper called him "The Dynamite King."
2. He became rich from his dynamite business.
3. (a) People used dynamite to build railroads, tunnels, dams, buildings, and roads.
   (b) because people needed a safe, powerful explosive for the railroads and tunnels they were beginning to build
4. (a) Yes, he did.
   (b) because he believed that if all countries had the same powerful weapons, they would see how impossible war was
5. Nobel read about Salomon August Andrée's expedition and had an inspiration. He wanted to encourage people to achieve.
6. He instructed people to use his money for an award to honor leaders of science, literature, and world peace.
7. Men or women of any nationality can receive prizes in the fields of physics, chemistry, medicine, literature, peace, and economics.
8. The world sees him as the creator of an important prize and as a man of peace.

### Exercise C

1. c
2. (a) 2
   (b) 1
3. b
4. c
5. c
6. (a) 2
   (b) 1
   (c) 3
7. c

8. (a) It is a legal statement telling how a person wishes his/her posses-
      sions to be distributed after death.
   (b) There is a star after **Last Will and Testament** that tells the reader to
      look at the bottom of the page for an explanation.
   (c) footnote
   (d) Last Will and Testament
9. (a) subjects; areas of study
   (b) physics, chemistry, medicine, literature
10. error

## Exercise D

**Part 1**
1. instructed / instructions
2. invented / inventions
3. construction / did not construct
4. inspired / inspiration
5. did not continue / continuation

**Part 2**
1. announced / announcement
2. did not excite / excitement
3. amazed / amazement
4. establishment / did not establish
5. statements / stated

## Exercise E

1. headline
2. perfect
3. peaceful
4. too
5. all the same
6. upset
7. nationality
8. violence
9. at all
10. mistake

## Exercise F

Answers will vary.

## Exercise G

Answers will vary.

## Exercise H

| Across Clues | Down Clues |
|---|---|
| 1. we | 1. will |
| 2. his | 2. headline |
| 4. nationality | 3. invent |
| 5. remember | 6. my |
| 7. our | 8. upset |
| 9. dynamite | 9. dangerous |
| 11. weapons | 10. field |
| 12. explosive | 13. peace |
| 16. award | 14. sure |
| 17. violence | 15. construct |
| 19. fortune | 18. he |
| 21. mistake | 20. him |

## Exercise I

1. read
2. was or became
3. had
4. thought
5. made
6. were or became
7. read
8. had
9. knew
10. wrote
11. was
12. had
13. were
14. read
15. became

---

# Chapter 12. Marie Curie: A 20th Century Woman

## Exercise A

1. T
2. F.   She was born in Poland.
3. F.   She went to the university in Paris.
4. T
5. T
6. T
7. F.   She was the first woman to receive the Nobel prize.

8. T
9. F.   She did not want to earn a lot of money.

## Exercise B

1. (a)  She was 23 years old.
   (b)  because she worked for six years to help her sister go to school
2. (a)  She met him in Paris.
   (b)  They both believed that science was the most important part of their lives, and they didn't care about money or about being comfortable.
3. They looked for unknown elements that gave off X rays.
4. (a)  They discovered polonium and radium.
   (b)  They received the Nobel prize in physics.
5. (a)  She isolated radium in 1910.
   (b)  She was the first woman to receive a doctor of science degree from the Sorbonne. She was the first woman to receive a Nobel prize. She was the first person to receive a Nobel prize twice.
6. (a)  She died On July 4, 1934.
   (b)  Exposure to radium caused her death.

## Exercise C

1. b
2. (a)  1
   (b)  3
   (c)  1
3. (a)  2
   (b)  1
   (c)  3
4. b
5. (a)  2
   (b)  1
   (c)  1
6. (a)  2
   (b)  3
7. (a)  They are invisible, high-energy forms of light that can pass through many solid objects.
   (b)  There is a star after **X ray** that tells the reader to look at the bottom of the page for an explanation.
   (c)  footnote
8. (a)  1
   (b)  3
9. a
10. polonium and radium
11. a

12. (a) 1
    (b) 2
    (c) 2
    (d) 1
13. b
14. (a) 2
    (b) 3

**Exercise D**

**Part 1**
1. occurrences / occurred
2. existence / existed
3. did not persevere / perseverance
4. assistance / assisted
5. did not assure / assurances

**Part 2**
1. ill / illnesses
2. great / greatness
3. happiness / happy
4. short /shortness
5. near / nearness

**Exercise E**

1. unfortunately
2. exposure
3. in spite of
4. in order to
5. achieved
6. interruptions
7. supported
8. discovery
9. finally
10. about to

**Exercise F**

Answers will vary.

**Exercise G**

Answers will vary.

## Exercise H

**Across Clues**

6. tragic
8. unfortunately
11. support
12. me
13. discovery
14. put
17. illness
18. hit
20. elements
22. no
23. exposure
26. finally

**Down Clues**

1. accomplishment
2. interruption
3. gone
4. run
5. perseverance
7. award
9. radioactive
10. lost
15. lent
16. dangerous
19. one
21. shown
24. up
25. all

## Exercise I

1. her
2. she
3. her
4. her
5. she
6. she
7. her
8. she
9. her
10. her
11. she
12. he
13. they
14. they
15. their
16. they
17. they
18. their
19. his
20. her
21. he
22. she